Reflective Learning

Unpacking key Christian beliefs in
RE and collective worship

Trevor Reader and Lilian Weatherley

To Lilian's son Stephen, and Trevor's daughters Sam, Krissie, Alex, Katie, Susie and Lucy for the constancy of their love, support and encouragement.

Acknowledgments

We should like to thank all those people who have given us so much help and support during the course of producing this book.

Bishop Kenneth Stevenson, who has written the foreword, and also for his constant encouragement.

Sally Read for her patience, understanding and invaluable administrative support.

Stephen Buckley for his artwork on creation.

The staff at the Southern Theological Education Training Scheme for the initial inspiration for the Silent Eucharist, which is outlined in this book.

The many teachers who have not only inspired us with their own creative ideas but have also trialled some of the material contained in this book.

Trevor Reader is the Archdeacon of Portsdown and Chairman of the Portsmouth Diocesan Board of Education. He was ordained in 1986, having previously worked as a researcher and senior lecturer in biological science for 21 years. Since ordination he has served in the Portsmouth diocese in parish ministry, as director of non-stipendiary ministry and, for the past six years, as Archdeacon. Trevor was married to a primary school teacher until her recent death, and nurturing a close relationship with primary schools has always been central to his ministry. As well as being a school governor, he has led both teacher and clergy training and worked extensively with Lilian Weatherley to produce materials for collective worship and the Eucharist in primary schools. Trevor and Lilian are co-authors of *Teaching Christianity at Key Stage 2* (CHP).

Lilian Weatherley is the Diocesan Religious Education/Schools' Adviser for the Diocese of Portsmouth and Winchester. After training and working as a primary school teacher for several years, Lilian moved into secondary education, where she taught Religious Education, Special Educational Needs English, Dance, Drama and Art. Lilian has considerable experience of in-service training in both primary and secondary schools as well as with parish clergy. She was formerly an OFSTED inspector and continues to inspect Section 48. Lilian has written a wide range of materials on Religious Education and collective worship, and also represents the National Society on the RE Council for England and Wales.

Text copyright © Trevor Reader and Lilian Weatherley 2009
Illustrations copyright © Paula Doherty 2009
The authors assert the moral right
to be identified as the authors of this work

Published by
The Bible Reading Fellowship
15 The Chambers, Vineyard
Abingdon OX14 3FE
United Kingdom
Tel: +44 (0)1865 319700
Email: enquiries@brf.org.uk
Website: www.brf.org.uk

ISBN 978 1 84101 573 6
First published 2009
10 9 8 7 6 5 4 3 2 1 0

Acknowledgments
Unless otherwise stated, scripture quotations are taken from the
Contemporary English Version of the Bible published by HarperCollins
Publishers, copyright © 1991, 1992, 1995 American Bible Society.

A catalogue record for this book is available from the British Library

Printed in Singapore by Craft Print International Ltd

Contents

Key Concept One:
Who God is: the concept of the Trinity

Key Concept Two:
What God has done: the concept of salvation

Key Concept Three:
The Church today: the concept of reflective living

Foreword

The significance of religion in today's world is often matched by an equally significant level of incomprehension. Schools play an essential part in preparing children and young people to appreciate the importance and value of their religious heritage and context. This book is specially designed to meet the needs of teachers, RE coordinators, clergy and others who have a commitment or responsibility to oversee this vital work. As you would expect, it contains a wealth of useful information and tried-and-tested advice. It also offers a joined-up approach that includes material for school worship, Religious Education and class-based reflection. But its greatest strength is the way the authors integrate ideas, experience and practice, making connections between school, home and community life. It is the fundamentally lived nature of religion that is usually hardest to capture in the classroom, and so I believe that in this book Trevor Reader and Lilian Weatherley have provided us with a resource of real and, to my knowledge, unique importance. I recommend it very warmly indeed.

The Rt Revd Dr Kenneth Stevenson, The Lord Bishop of Portsmouth

✤

Introduction

Religious Education provokes challenging questions about the ultimate meaning and purpose of life, beliefs about God, the self and the nature of reality, issues of right and wrong and what it means to be human. It develops pupils' knowledge and understanding of Christianity, other principal religions, other traditions and other worldviews.
NON-STATUTORY FRAMEWORK FOR RELIGIOUS EDUCATION 2004

In 2004 the arrival of the new non-statutory framework for Religious Education prompted each Standing Advisory Council for Religious Education (SACRE) to consider the importance of the subject, re-evaluate their current agreed syllabus and analyse how the subject was taught in order to engage pupils in their learning and raise standards.

Reflective Learning aims to provide teachers with background information relating to key Christian beliefs and concepts in an attempt to give them more confidence in the subject matter. The material offers important tools to enable teachers to teach Christian beliefs and concepts in the light of biblical teaching and contemporary living and to undertake this teaching with confidence.

In recent years the revolution in the primary school classroom with the use of ICT has given teachers and pupils access to a wealth of material. With the press of a button pupils can now explore ways in which artists and musicians throughout the centuries and across the world have expressed their faith and belief. Throughout the world the creative arts have been fundamental to the world of religion and spirituality.

Pupils now have opportunities to investigate, analyse and evaluate aspects of religious belief and practice, as well as opportunities to develop their own spirituality. This book focuses on helping pupils engage with the Christian tradition and develop their knowledge and understanding of key Christian concepts and ideas in a creative and inspiring way, through the use of interactive whiteboards, the Internet and the sensory curriculum. Furthermore, creative ideas are also provided for delivery of collective worship, and it is hoped that these will be used imaginatively.

Although the primary focus is on the beliefs and practices of the Church of England, we have attempted to include a range of Christian denominations where appropriate, so that they can be compared and contrasted. This is a key element of the majority of agreed syllabus documents and a key skill for more able pupils.

The book focuses on three key concepts related to the principal beliefs of the Christian faith: 'Who God is' (the concept of the Trinity), 'What God has done' (the concept of salvation) and 'The Church today' (the concept of reflective living). Each of the concepts is explored in relation to particular units of work as follows:

1 Trinity (who God is): The units are the stories of creation, re-creation and baptism.
2 Salvation (what God has done): The units are the stories of Christmas and Epiphany, Lent, Holy Week, Easter and Pentecost.
3 Church (reflective living): There are three units relating to the journey of life. They are 'Belonging and believing', 'Sharing and caring' and 'Patterns for living'.

In order to ground the teaching, each of these eleven units explores its theme following a common format as follows:

○ Background information for the teacher: This provides a theological basis for the unit that follows and some key facts to help the teacher.
○ Exploring the story: Here the biblical accounts relating to the unit are presented and examined.
○ Introductory questions about the story: Here are some initial questions to stimulate the children to unpack the story.

- Introductory tasks: These are designed not only to get the children to dig deeper into the story but also to help them think both laterally and creatively.
- Key symbols in the story: Bible stories are often rich in symbolism, and understanding this symbolism can be the key to unpacking the story in an exciting way for children.
- Understanding the story through the senses: The story is considered in relation to each of the senses—sight, sound, smell, touch and taste. With respect to the sense of sight, the unit always includes reference to a piece of well-known artwork on the subject. This artwork is intended to provide a significant focus for both classroom study and school worship. Each piece of artwork chosen can easily be found on the Internet using a web search engine.
- A focus table of reflection for the classroom: Here are some creative ideas reflecting the theme of the unit, which can provide a basis for classroom worship or continued reflection on the theme. It is hoped that the focus table will help pupils develop an awareness of awe and wonder within daily living and the school environment.
- Reflecting on the story: This section comprises two acts of collective worship for assembly, each of which follows a common format and includes:
  - a list of things that are needed for the worship
  - suggestions for opening music and entrance
  - a Christian greeting
  - an introduction for the leader
  - an 'application' that provides the basis for the talk
  - a prayer
  - suggestions for songs
  - a dismissal
  - suggestions for music to exit
  - two 'optional extras' to give the teacher even more variety and choice

All the suggested images for study and collective worship are readily available on the Internet. You will need a projector (or laptop) and a screen to display the images in collective worship and the classroom. In collective worship, you may also wish to display the response for the Christian greetings and dismissals.

All of the recorded music suggested for entrances and exits, and for 'Understanding the story through the senses', is available on CD. The Resources section (pp. 184–187) gives details of recommended sources, although some of the pieces can be found on many different recordings.

All the songs suggested for collective worship can be found in the following resource books. See page 187 for publishing details.

- ❂ Church Family Worship (CFW)
- ❂ Hymns Old and New (HON)
- ❂ Mission Praise (MP)
- ❂ Wild Goose Songs (WGS)

Who God is:
The concept of the Trinity

Christians regard their religion as monotheistic, since Christianity teaches the existence of one God. It shares this belief with two other major world religions: Judaism and Islam. However, Christian monotheism is a unique kind of monotheism. It holds that God is one, but that three distinct 'persons' constitute the one God—the Father, the Son and the Holy Spirit. This unique threefold God of Christian belief is referred to as the Trinity (from Latin *trinitas* meaning 'triad').

Belief in the Trinity finds expression in the creeds of the Christian Church. Christians declare:

We believe in one God, the Father, the almighty, maker of heaven and earth... We believe in one Lord Jesus Christ, the only Son of God... for our salvation he came down from heaven... We believe in the Holy Spirit, the Lord the giver of life, who proceeds from the Father and the Son.

In this section of the book we shall be looking at these three persons of the Trinity: Father, Son and Holy Spirit.

In relation to God the Father, we shall concentrate on the story of creation, since Christians believe that God is the creator of all that is, including human beings, who are described as being made 'in the image of God' (Genesis 1:27, TNIV).

Then, in relation to Jesus Christ, we shall consider his pivotal significance for Christians with regard to re-creation. Christians believe that re-creation is necessary because although, when God the Father created the world, he saw that it was good, creation was marred by the constant disobedience of human beings. The consequence of this disobedience was, and is, separation from God. Christians believe that Jesus came into the world to show us how we can be forgiven for all the things that break our relationship with God and thereby be reconciled with God. In this way we can be recreated in the image of God.

In relation to the Holy Spirit, the book will concentrate on how Christians believe that he gives new life to the people of God. The key focus here will be on baptism, since this is regarded as the pivotal means by which individuals receive new life in Christ. We will see in Jesus' own baptism the key role that the Holy Spirit plays. Thus, John the Baptist, who performed Jesus' baptism, declared, 'The one who sent me to baptize with water had told me, "You will see the Spirit come down and stay on someone. Then you will know that he is the one who will baptize with the Holy Spirit." I saw this happen, and I tell you that he is the Son of God' (John 1:33–34). Other aspects of the life-giving work of the Holy Spirit, such as the giving of gifts or the fruit of the Spirit, will be considered separately in the later chapter on Pentecost.

A useful image for the concept of the Trinity is the 15th-century icon by Andrej Rublev, *The Hospitality of Abraham*.

The story of creation

Background information for the teacher

Christians generally view creation as being the loving act of God by which the universe came into being, but it is more than that. It also means sustaining and nurturing everything that has been created, so there is a continuum to creation.

Probably the best-known biblical account of creation is to be found in the book of Genesis (especially Genesis 1:1—2:4) but there are others, such as Genesis 2:4–25, Job 38—41 and Psalm 104.

The fundamental Christian understanding at the heart of each of these creation stories is that God created everything, of his own free will, out of nothing, and that human beings were given a pivotal place in that creation.

What is also clear is that over the centuries there have been a variety of interpretations of creation. For example, some prefer to see creation as a one-off event, while others perceive it as an unfolding drama with a constant stream of new opportunities and fresh discoveries. Some Christians (known as creationists) prefer to accept the biblical account of creation in Genesis 1 as being literally true rather than accepting the theory of evolution.

It is clear that the debate surrounding these different interpretations cannot be resolved by appeal to any one particular account of creation in the Bible. What these accounts do emphasize, however, is that God is the author of the story of creation; this is a fundamental Christian belief. If there is a design to the created order, then Christians believe that God is the designer.

The biblical stories of creation are also important because they enable us to have a better understanding of the universe and of our place within it. If human beings have been created by God for a special divine–human relationship, it is also apparent that this brings a range of responsibilities. The dominion given to humans over the rest of the created order expressed in Genesis 1:26 has been interpreted by some as giving humans freedom to do what they want with the rest of creation—a despotic dominion. Others have preferred to interpret it as emphasizing our responsibility in being 'stewards of creation'; thus human beings have a real responsibility in relation to such issues as global warming, protection of species and so on.

Exploring the story

For centuries people have tried to make sense of how life began. Stories have been passed down from generation to generation. The stories in Genesis are at the heart of the Judeo-Christian tradition, which believes that all life began with God. In Genesis 1, we read that God created the universe in seven days. By exploring each day it is possible to see the developmental pattern of creation.

Day 1: God created light and darkness.
Day 2: God separated waters from waters.
Day 3: God separated the land from the sea and created vegetation, seeds, plants and trees.
Day 4: God created the stars, sun and moon, day and night.
Day 5: God created the creatures of the sea and air.
Day 6: God created the creatures of the earth.
Day 7: God rested.

Most scientists today say that the solar system was formed 4.6 billion years ago by clouds of gas and solids joining together and rotating around the sun to form planets. There is a difference between these two timescales of seven days and 4.6 billion years! People often argue about the meaning of the word 'day' in Genesis 1—whether it means '24 hours' or whether it is a way of suggesting the process of creation rather than its exact timing. But, although the book of Genesis was not an attempt to give a 'scientific' explanation, the account in Genesis 1 certainly indicates that the people of the Old Testament were not far out in their ordering of creation, considering their lack of scientific knowledge.

Introductory questions about the story

Find out about scientific viewpoints of how the world was formed. Read Genesis 1:1—2:4 and Genesis 2:5–25. Do you think that the scientific and biblical views are contradictory or is the biblical view a more poetic way of saying the same thing?

Introductory tasks

☺ Compare the creation story in Genesis 1:1—2:4 with the story in Genesis 2:5–25. What are the similarities and the differences?
☺ Read Psalm 148. Write your own poem based on the story of creation.
☺ Read Genesis 1:28. This verse talks about people ruling over all other living creatures. Imagine you were God. Write a list of instructions for the human race in order to ensure that people look after and protect what you have created.
☺ Explore some creation stories from other faith traditions. What are the similarities and the differences?

Key symbols in the story

The Spirit of God

The Spirit of God usually refers to the power and energy of God. The word 'spirit' comes from the Hebrew word *ruach* and refers to the life-giving breath of God. In the Genesis story we hear about the power of God moving over the waters.

The heavens

When the story begins, there is no form to anything—just darkness—but the Spirit of God moves across the darkness and separates the light from the dark. The story tells how, on the second day, God created a firmament that divided waters from waters. The firmament was called heaven. Into this God placed two great lights—the sun and the moon to light the sky—as well as the stars. A night sky is symbolic of the vastness of God's created order.

The physical world

The writers of the book of Genesis would have had a very different view of the earth from the view we have today. For example, they would have thought that the earth was flat. It is worth remembering this when reading these stories. The diagram on the following page gives a Western medieval view of the world in the Genesis story.

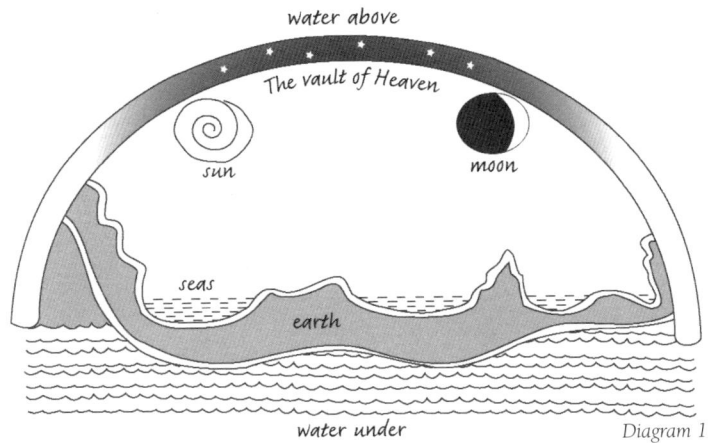

water above

The vault of Heaven

sun

moon

seas

earth

water under

Diagram 1

Plant life

The story does not just talk about vegetation, but also about seeds (Genesis 1:11). It is clear that the created plant life was to continue and to flourish. Trees were always a key symbol of life in the Jewish tradition as they were an important source of life, providing food, firewood and other resources. If trees did not grow, they were also a symbol of death. Genesis 2:9 speaks of two trees: one with the power to give life, and the other giving power to know what is right and wrong. These have become key symbols in the Christian tradition.

Animal life

Animal life begins with the sea creatures and then the other animals and creatures. The myriad of species created reminds us of the bounty of God's creation, which is symbolic of his creativity.

Human life

The word Adam means 'first man'. The story also says that 'God created humans to be like himself' (1:27). It is this phrase that has prompted artists throughout the generations to paint God in human form, often like an old man with a long white beard. It is worth reflecting that although there is a vast variety of human ethnic groups, each person is unique (for example, each has his or her own fingerprints). Christians believe that each person is special in the eyes of God, and has been given individual responsibility to care for others and the rest of creation.

Understanding the story through the senses

Imagine that you were the first human being created. How important would your senses—sight, hearing, smell, touch and taste—have been for your appreciation of the rest of creation? Remember that God created these amazing senses to enable us to engage more effectively with all that he created.

Sight

Obtain an image of *Creation of the Animals* by Tintoretto. This can be found on the Internet using a web search engine. What do you think is happening in the painting? There is so much to see. Look closely at the picture. The artist has tried to capture the moment when God created the creatures. You can see the fish of the sea, the birds of the air and the beasts of the earth. God is shown in a blaze of light. Can you think why this might be? Do you think that the artist has captured the Spirit of God in this painting? How many different creatures can you see?

The artist has positioned the stick to make it look as if God is shooting the creatures at speed, as if from a bow and arrow. In Genesis 9:9–17 God talks about setting a rainbow in the sky as a sign of his solemn promise to all living creatures on the earth. If you look carefully at the hand of God in the painting, you can see that the finger is pointed in the same way that Michelangelo Buonarroti portrayed the hand of God in his painting of creation in the Sistine Chapel in Rome, at an earlier date.

There is also a tree on the right hand of the painting. This looks very much like an olive tree. If you read the story of Noah in Genesis 8:6–12, you can see that the dove returned with a green leaf from an olive tree in its beak, to show that the waters of the flood had dried up and the earth was once again habitable. The olive was an important tree as it gave oil for light and healing, wood for fire and fruit to eat.

You might also consider what sights would have amazed you had you been the first living human on earth.

Sound

Our ears are very sensitive organs. When they send signals to our brain, the brain compares the sounds with other sounds and helps us to understand what we have heard. Sit quietly and reflect on the silence. Is it possible to have silence in today's world? Imagine the silence and then those first murmurs of creation, or the sounds that the first human beings would have heard. What sound would you miss if you lost your sense of hearing?

Listen carefully to the words of the hymn 'Think of a world without any flowers' and reflect on their significance.

Smell

The nose is a very important organ in the body. As we breathe air in and out, the nose is able to smell different scents. Imagine that you were without the sense of smell. Can you think of any advantages and disadvantages that this might present in your life? What smells would you miss the most in the natural, created world?

Touch

Inside the skin are thousands of tiny nerve endings or receptors. They measure heat, cold, pain and pressure, and send signals to the brain so that even if a tiny insect crawls up your arm you know it is there.

How important is our sense of touch? Compare the touch of a shiny apple with a pineapple, or a pebble with a pine cone. Close your eyes and feel the differences in texture—rough or smooth, hard or soft, light or heavy, hot or cold, small or large, wet or dry. Now take off your shoes. Imagine how the first human beings felt, walking on the earth, or on sand, or on grass. If you were the first human, what might be the first thing that you would like to touch? Could it be your own skin?

Taste

The tongue has tiny taste buds to help us distinguish foods. There are four main tastes: sweet, sour, bitter and salty. You might try to taste some lemon and honey, or some olives or bitter herbs and some salt.

Genesis 3 goes on to tell the story of how Adam and Eve were tempted to eat the fruit from the tree that they had been told not to touch. Have you ever eaten something that you were told not to touch? Sometimes food can look so inviting that it is hard to resist. Think how different our world might be to us if we were unable to taste food.

A focus table of reflection for the classroom

Prepare a table with a candle in the centre. Divide the table into two sides using two different coloured cloths (one to represent God's creation and one to represent people's misuses of the earth). Use photographic images from the Internet or magazines, or artefacts, to depict each item.

Design one side to reflect the six days of the creation story:

❂ Day and night
❂ Sea and sky

- A globe to represent the earth and plant life
- The sun, moon and stars
- Sea creatures and birds of the air
- Creatures of the land and human beings
- A copy of Psalm 148

Design the other side to reflect what is happening to the earth today, such as:

- Oiled birds
- Litter
- Global warming
- Deserts
- Dead plant life
- Graffiti

Each day, light the candle to represent the creation of the earth. Have available an empty basket and a supply of pebbles. Ask the pupils to reflect on the contrast between the two sides of the table and then to offer a prayer to God for the future of the planet by placing a pebble in the basket on the table.

Reflecting on the story

Assembly One: The universe

The following outline will enable the children to take a journey through the universe. As a consequence they should appreciate the awe and wonder of creation, as well as the place of the earth within the whole created order.

You will need:

❖ A table with a cloth, a candle and a globe.

❖ A sound recording of the first landing on the moon: 'One small step for a man, one giant leap for mankind' (Search on Google: "Neil Armstrong's moon landing").

❖ Satellite images of a local street, town, country, Europe, the world (available from Google Earth).

❖ Images of the earth taken from the surface of the moon (search www.nasaimages.org).

❖ Images of the planets (search www.nasaimages.org).

❖ Images of another galaxy such as the Milky Way (search www.nasaimages.org).

❖ Image from the Hubble deep field telescope showing innumerable galaxies.
(See http://hubblesite.org/gallery/album/entire_collection/pr1996001a/).

❖ An image from the Voyager One spacecraft 1990, showing the most distant picture of the earth ever taken—from four billion miles away.
(See http://fullygeek.com/wp-content/uploads/2006/11/bluedot.jpg)

To accompany the Voyager One image, you will need a speech by the astronomer Carl Sagan, entitled 'The pale blue dot'. The text of this speech can be obtained on Wikipedia, and an audio recording is also available on YouTube. Both are available via an Internet search engine.

The speech reminds us that the pale blue dot in the Voyager One image is the earth—our home—and goes on to say that this insignificant dot has been home to every human being who has ever lived. Sagan then challenges us to reflect upon all the horrific things that humankind has done upon the earth, before reminding us that our very survival is up to us. The responsibility rests with us. We must cherish that pale blue dot, for it is the only home we've ever known.

Suggested opening music and entrance

✪ *Also Sprach Zarathustra* by Richard Strauss (used in the Stanley Kubrick film *2001: A Space Odyssey*)

A Christian greeting

Leader: Come, let us praise God who made heaven and earth.
Response: And give thanks for the wonders of his creation.

Introduction

Remind the children of what happened on day four of the creation story (Genesis 1:14–19). Explain that you are now going to take them on a journey from a well-known local street to the most distant parts of the universe.

Suggested songs

O praise ye the Lord (HON 388)
All creatures of our God and King (omit verses 5 and 6) (HON 9)
Who put the colours in the rainbow? (HON 557)

Application

Using the satellite images, take the children on a journey into space beginning with a well-known local street and then going on to the local town, country, continent and world.

Next, show an image of the earth taken from the Apollo craft Voyager One after it landed on the moon. Explain that this is the furthest any person has ever travelled. Play the recording of Neil Armstrong's famous speech as he stepped on to the moon's surface.

Now, using more images, take the children on a journey into outer space, viewing each of the planets in sequence. (This could be accompanied by more music from *Also Sprach Zarathustra*.)

Then show them a galaxy such as the Milky Way, followed by the image from the Hubble deep field telescope of innumerable galaxies. Remind the children that, for this last image, astronomers chose the emptiest part of the sky and looked at it for ten days. This is the image they found. The picture shows 3000 galaxies, with approximately 30,000,000,000,000 stars like our own sun. The area of sky covered by this picture is the same size as a grain of sand. Pause to appreciate the awe and wonder of God's creation.

Now show the image from the Voyager One spacecraft which is the most distant picture ever taken of the earth, taken from 4 billion miles away. The earth is seen as a minute blue speck.

As they look closely at this image, read them the speech by Carl Sagan. Remind the children of the Christian belief that God visited that tiny spot as Jesus, born in a stable in Bethlehem. Christians believe that we are not alone. God is here; his Spirit is with us.

Prayer

Dear God, we thank you for the beauty and wonder of the universe, particularly for our own solar system, and for the skills and knowledge of astronomers, scientists and engineers who have made it possible for us to explore this majestic part of your creation. We thank you for the great courage and skills of astronauts who have journeyed through space to bring us fresh knowledge, a deeper understanding and a more vibrant appreciation of the beauty of our solar system. We pray for all those who are currently involved in space research and exploration. Help us never to lose our sense of awe and wonder in relation to our solar system as we share life together on this planet.

(Light a candle) We praise you, God, for your great and mighty wonders of creation—for things we are able to see and understand and for those things that have not yet been revealed to us. Amen

Dismissal

Leader: Shout for joy to the Lord, all the earth.
Response: Serve the Lord with gladness.

Suggested music to exit

The children leave to more music from *Also Sprach Zarathustra* by Richard Strauss.

Optional extras

1 Prayer bubbles are most appropriate. Blow bubbles and ask children to quietly 'place' their prayers into a bubble. Christians believe that God hears these prayers. Ask the children to imagine their prayers being released to God as each bubble bursts.
2 Children could be dressed up as the sun and planets (or hold large images of them). As an image of each planet is revealed on the screen, the children are arranged in precise formation around the sun. Choose children of different heights to emphasize the difference in the size of the planets and so on.

Assembly Two: Our responsibility towards God's world

The following outline will emphasize the difference between all that is good and all that is bad in our world. Children will be encouraged to see that, with God's help, they can make a difference.

You will need:
+ Images of the earth from outer space (available on Google). Find images of the earth from a distance, but also closer images of Europe, United Kingdom, your county, your town, your street.
+ Images to illustrate current problems with the world (motor vehicles and other aspects of pollution, wars and other hostilities, deforestation, global warming, sickness and so on).

❖ Images illustrating examples of positive responses to these problems and of hope (research workers in medical laboratories, medical staff, charitable relief to famine, newborn babies, children playing and laughing together and so on).

❖ A table with a candle and a globe.

Suggested opening music and entrance

⊙ 'Morning mood' from *Peer Gynt Suite No. 1*, Opus 46 by Edvard Grieg

⊙ Music from Part 1 of *The Creation* by Franz Joseph Haydn

As children enter, an image of the world is shown on screen.

Christian greeting

Leader: Let us rejoice in God's world.
Response: And care for his creation.

Introduction

Read to the children Genesis 1:31: 'God looked at what he had done. All of it was very good!' Explain that they will now see contrasting images, reminding us of the ways in which people have either spoilt or helped God's creation. Encourage them to consider what they can do to make a difference in rebuilding those parts of God's world that have been spoilt.

Suggested song

He's got the whole world in his hands (HON 206)

Application

Show an image of the earth from outer space. Give the children time to appreciate its beauty, and the opportunity to identify continents and oceans.

Gradually zoom in on the earth, using further images to reveal Europe, the UK, your county, town and street. Remind the children that this is where they live on God's earth. Ask them to reflect on whether or not this is a place of beauty. Would God say of their street, 'God looked at what he had done and all of it was very good'?

Using the various negative images, consider what people have done to mar God's creation. Invite the children to offer suggestions on other aspects of misusing God's world that they are concerned about.

Now, using the various positive images, consider examples of ways in which people have responded positively to these problems. Invite the children to offer suggestions about other ways in which people help to care for and rebuild those parts of God's world that have been spoilt.

Return to the image of your local town or street. Encourage the children to consider the ways in which they can make a difference to the world they know. Help them to see that they really can make a difference to the bit of God's world that they are standing on (no one else inhabits that bit of God's world). Encourage the children to think about:

❂ Avoiding vandalism and pollution (challenging the throwaway society we live in).
❂ Recycling of materials.
❂ Saving energy (turning off lights when they are not in use, not using 'standby' buttons, and so on).
❂ Providing peace and harmony in their personal relationships, and so on.

Now zoom outwards from the earth to the distant view from space. Express the hope that our world will remain just as beautiful and full of love for generations to come. Repeat, 'God looked at what he had done. All of it was very good!'

Prayer

Light the candle by the globe.

Dear God, we thank you for our wonderful world, which you have created out of love—for light and darkness; sky and sea; land, plants, flowers and fruit; the sun, moon and stars; the fish of the sea and birds of the air; animals and insects; men, women, boys and girls, and for all that makes life on this earth so good. Help us to do our best to care for your world. Forgive us when we spoil it, and guide us as we play our part in rebuilding those parts that have been spoilt. Amen

Dismissal

Leader: Shout for joy to the Lord, all the earth!
Response: Serve the Lord with gladness!

Suggested music to exit

Children leave to a recording of 'All things bright and beautiful' arranged by John Rutter.

Optional extras

1 Ask the children to vote on their top ten problems facing the world.
2 Ask the children to vote on their top ten things they can do to help in God's world.

The story of re-creation

Background information for the teacher

In the preceding unit on creation, we saw how Christians believe that, out of love, God created human beings in his own image as the pinnacle of his creation. However, the story of Adam and Eve in Genesis 2 and 3 tells of the 'fall' of humanity from this privileged position.

Christians believe that this was not how God had meant it to be, but the story of Adam and Eve's disobedience to God highlights the fact that wrongdoing, which Christians call 'sin', has become deep-rooted in the world. However, the Bible shows us that God has never given up on his creation and never will. This is made clear very early in the story of Noah and his ark (Genesis 6—9), and through the promises to Abraham (Genesis 12:1; 15:1–6) and Moses (Exodus 6:1–6).

Later on, the Bible shows us that it was the prophets' responsibility to continue to give God's promise, or 'covenant', to his people. This often meant declaring God's verdict on the state of the world but also emphasizing what God would do now and in the future to draw people back to his ways—that is to say, to 're-create' them in his image. The message of the Old Testament prophets, and later John the Baptist, is a firm expression of God's determination never to give up on human beings.

Unfortunately, while many people listened, others failed to hear, and so throughout the story of the Old Testament we hear the constant story of men and women continuing to turn their backs on God. Thus re-creation was incomplete. However, throughout this troublesome history of Israel, there grew a hope among God's faithful people that one day God would send a Messiah—God's chosen one—to sort things out once and for all. This was the messianic hope of a divinely commissioned figure who would restore the world to the way it should be. Christians believe that this messianic hope found its fulfilment through the birth of Jesus Christ. God was finally reconciling himself with the world in the person of Jesus.

This is the concept of salvation. Thus God the Father is creator, but through his Son Jesus Christ he offers the possibility of re-creation and the opportunity to be at one with him again. By faith in Jesus Christ, Christians believe that they can turn back to God and be recreated afresh in his image.

This belief that Jesus is indeed the Saviour of the world is expressed in the Christian creed through the words, 'For us and for our salvation he came down from heaven'. Christians believe that this free gift is offered to all who believe that Jesus is the Son of God.

Exploring the story

This is a story that moves throughout time, a story made up of different chapters building up over centuries. It begins with the story of Adam and Eve in Genesis, and moves on through the story of Noah to the stories of Moses, Abraham, Jacob and Joseph. We then see God's revelations to those who were faithful to him throughout the Old Testament, including the prophets, and onward into the New Testament to Jesus' life: his incarnation, death and resurrection.

Read the story in Genesis 2:15—3:24 of Adam and Eve's disobedience to God and how they were sent out of the garden of

Eden. The story tells how God told Adam that he could eat from any of the trees in the garden except the tree with 'the power to let you know the difference between right and wrong' (2:17). The serpent, however, is seen to question God's authority and persuades Eve that she will not be harmed if she eats the fruit of the tree. Eve eats the fruit and then gives some to Adam. Consequently, both of them have disobeyed God. Christians call such wrongdoing 'sin'. In the story we find that God then punishes all three. First of all, the serpent will crawl on its stomach and eat dust, then the woman will experience suffering in childbirth, and then man will have to sweat to earn a living. Adam and Eve are sent out of the garden and told that they will never be allowed to return. They are to be cut off from God. Christians believe that it is 'sin' that separates people from God.

The story of Noah in Genesis 6—9 shows that, after Adam and Eve, things went from bad to worse. Noah and his family were saved from the great flood because Noah was the only person who 'lived right and obeyed God' (6:9). Having decided that his creation has been disobedient and all deserve extinction, God tells Noah to build an ark. Then God sends a flood to drown all living creatures but, because of Noah, a new beginning is possible. After Noah and the animals have spent months in the ark, dry land appears. The dove that Noah sends out returns with an olive leaf, which shows that the land is finally habitable.

In this story, God makes a promise or 'covenant' with Noah that he will never flood the earth again. Although the chance of paradise was lost in the Adam and Eve story, God has saved Noah and the animals and gives them a second chance. In Genesis 9:16 the rainbow in the story symbolizes better things to come. It is a sign of God's mercy and promise to every living creature.

Christians believe that, throughout the Old Testament, the history of Israel and the teachings of the prophets, God continued to renew his promise. Christians believe that it is a history that shows God's love for his creation from generation to generation. God is like a loving parent, trying to encourage his children to behave in the right way. He instructs, guides and pardons in an attempt to help people be the best they can be, but throughout the centuries people continue to make mistakes. They are like small children in a family—quarrelling, fighting and hurting each other, and often not listening to the parent who knows what is best for them.

Christians believe that the final part of the story is when God himself became a human being in the person of Jesus. Read the story in Luke 2:21–35. It tells how Mary and Joseph took Jesus, as an eight-day-old baby, to the temple to be circumcised. (Circumcision marks the entry of Jewish males into the 'covenant' between God and the Jewish people.) It is at this point that the elderly man Simeon recognizes Jesus as the longed-for Messiah. Christians see this as God finally reconciling himself with the world, in the person of Jesus.

In the Gospels we read how Jesus showed compassion and love to those whom others rejected. In the end, Jesus himself was rejected, betrayed, denied, arrested, mocked, scorned, tortured and crucified. Yet, in spite of all the pain inflicted upon him, Jesus never stopped loving those who persecuted him. For Christians, Jesus' death on the cross reveals God's perfect love.

Introductory questions about the story

If you were God, what would you want to say to humanity to help them learn from the history of their ancestors?

Introductory tasks

❂ Explore Christian art that depicts the story of Simeon in the temple (for example, *Presentation at the temple* by Giovanni Bellini. Imagine you were a newspaper reporter at the event.

Write your report and explain why, for Christians, Simeon's words are so important in the story of re-creation.

○ Imagine you were asked to write a story about human beings turning away from God and paradise today. What advice would you want to include in your story for people today?

○ Find out how the 'presentation of Christ in the temple' is celebrated in Christian churches worldwide.

Key symbols in the story

The tree of the knowledge of good and evil

This is sometimes referred to as the 'tree of conscience'. God told Adam and Eve that they could eat from any tree except this one. Having tasted the fruit, they became aware of their nakedness for the first time. It has always been a symbol of 'free choice' and what Christians call 'original sin'.

The fig leaf

This symbolizes the fact that both man and woman now recognize their nakedness, that they are no longer at ease in each other's company. It is also a symbol of separation from God as a result of disobedience.

The serpent

Serpents are often connected with deceit. This idea may depend in part on the observation that snakes often have forked tongues. In humans, the presence of only one tip to the tongue signifies the unity of truthful speech. In contrast, a forked tongue represents the disunity of deceitful speech. In the story, the serpent is the perfect symbol of temptation; it acts as the devil in disguise and persuades Adam and Eve to disobey God's warning.

The ark

The ark in this story is a huge boat about the size of the *Titanic*. It is a symbol of God's continuing love for human beings and is a sign of his presence with his people. It is also a reminder that God longs to save his people.

The raven

This bird is a scavenger and, in Judaism, is regarded as unclean. It is therefore a symbol of things that are rotten in our world.

The dove

The dove is a symbol of the power of God—a symbol of the Holy Spirit. In the story of Noah, the dove does not leave the ark permanently until the green growth on the land has returned. It then returns with an olive branch. So, it is also a symbol of hope.

The olive branch

Like the dove, this has become a symbol of peace and harmony. Tranquillity and peace had been restored to the land following the disruption of the flood.

The rainbow

The rainbow is God's promise of better things to come. It replaces the fighting bow used in war. It is a sign of God's mercy and marks the covenant of God's peace with humanity.

Understanding the story through the senses

Christians believe that God's covenant relationship with humanity found fulfilment in the life and person of Jesus. Whereas in the Old Testament we see God revealing his love primarily through speaking and listening, in Jesus all of the senses are involved.

Sight

In Colossians 1:15, Paul says that Jesus is 'exactly like God, who cannot be seen'. Look closely at a picture of *Presentation of Jesus in the Temple* by Vittore Carpaccio. This can be found on the Internet using a web search engine. It depicts the story from Luke 2:22–35, when Mary and Joseph took Jesus when he was eight days old to the temple to be circumcised. Read the story and then look at the picture.

Luke records how the Holy Spirit had told Simeon that he would see the Messiah before he died. Here the artist has tried to capture the moment when Simeon sees the child and recognizes him. Look closely at the elderly man's face and the light reflected on the child. Christians across the world celebrate this event on 2 February. The festival is called Candlemas.

Sound

Listen to a recording of Simeon's words, called the Nunc Dimittis (see Resources section, p. 184). These words are often sung in Christian churches to remind Christians of the event. Also consider some of the words that Jesus himself spoke. For example, listen to the words of the Lord's Prayer (Matthew 6:9–13). What is Jesus trying to say about God and his kingdom? Look at the words from the hymn 'Shine, Jesus, shine' by Graham Kendrick (HON 317). Write some new words for it, to reflect Jesus being the light for the world.

Smell

In 2 Corinthians 2:14, Paul refers to the knowledge about Christ as being like the smell of perfumes. Then, in verse 15, he says, 'God thinks of us as a perfume that brings Christ to everyone. For people who are being saved, this perfume has a sweet smell and leads them to a better life.'

Touch

The sense of touch is clearly present in Jesus' healing miracles. For example, read Luke 4:40: 'After the sun had set, people with all kinds of diseases were brought to Jesus. He put his hands on each one of them and healed them.'

Taste

Jesus referred to himself as bread (John 6:35). At the last supper, he referred to the bread and wine of Passover as his body and his blood (Mark 14:22–24).

A focus table of reflection for the classroom

The story of re-creation takes place over many centuries. It begins with the creation story and continues through the Old Testament until the birth of Jesus. Prepare a table about re-creation by placing seven candles of differing sizes, gradually getting larger until the sixth candle. This sixth candle represents Jesus. Place a smaller seventh candle beside the sixth candle. This candle represents us. Point out that the seven candles also link back to the seven days of creation. Place a copy of the prayer of Francis of Assisi (which begins 'Lord, make me an instrument of your peace') on the table.

Each day, over seven consecutive days, light a new candle. The seven days symbolize:

1 Adam and Eve, the first man and woman
2 Noah and his family
3 Abraham
4 Moses
5 The Old Testament prophets
6 Jesus
7 Ourselves

Each day, as a candle is lit, think about the ways in which Christians believe that we have turned away from God and how God has never given up on us. Throughout history, God has sent someone to try to teach people how to live in the right way.

As each new candle is lit, read the words of St Francis' prayer. Alternatively, use the prayer below.

Prayer

Dear God, may we always look out for ways in which we can do good, so that we may help the world become a better place. Amen

Optional extra

The following optional extra is designed to help the children to understand the Christian belief that we are known personally by God and that God never gives up on us.

On the first day, give each pupil a large pebble. Ask them to look at their pebble very carefully and to note its particular features, such as its shape, size, colour, grains and so on. Let them keep this pebble for seven days, each day examining it closely. On the seventh day, place a large tray on the floor and ask the children to place their pebbles on the tray. Mix the pebbles up. Then ask the children to find their particular pebble. Explain how this reminds us that

Christians believe that God knows and loves each one of us individually (just as they have got to know the pebble individually). Light the seventh candle, which is for ourselves. The children could then take home their pebble as a keepsake.

Reflecting on the story

Assembly One: The parable of the lost son

The following outline helps pupils to appreciate that we can always turn back to God for forgiveness, whatever the circumstances.

You will need:
- ✤ A table with a candle.
- ✤ A narrator to read the story from Luke 15:11–32.
- ✤ Characters for the father, younger son, older son, partygoers, pigs and servants (all dressed appropriately).
- ✤ A bag of money, robes, sandals, a ring and a garden spade.
- ✤ An image of the prodigal son, such as Rembrandt's *The Return of the Prodigal Son*.

Suggested opening music and entrance

Children enter to a recording of a song or hymn about God the Father, such as:

○ Abba, Father
○ Dear Lord and Father of mankind

Project the chosen image on a screen.

Christian greeting

Leader: Come, let us praise God our Father.
Response: He alone does marvellous things.

Introduction

Refer to the image on the screen. Ask the children if they know the story it is based on. Explain to the children that they are now going to see a dramatized presentation of Jesus' parable about the lost son. This is sometimes called the parable of the prodigal son. Explain that a parable is a story of everyday life that Jesus told, which had a deeper spiritual meaning. There are over 30 parables to be found in the Gospels.

Suggested song

Sing a hymn or song that focuses on either forgiveness or love, or a song about journeying through life. For example:

- ❂ God forgave my sin in Jesus' name (HON 16)
- ❂ The King of Love my shepherd is (HON 484)
- ❂ One more step (HON 405)

Application

As the narrator reads the story, the children mime the drama, using the various props. It begins with the younger son asking the father for money. The father gives his son the money bag and the son leaves home (*go to the other end of the hall*). The father stays at home. The younger son enjoys partying with friends (*act out party*) and spends all the money (*bag empty*). When all the money is gone, he goes to a farm, where he looks after pigs and is so hungry that he eats their food (*younger son crawls around an imaginary feeding trough with the pigs*). The younger son comes to his senses and rushes home. His father spots him and runs to meet him. They embrace and the son is taken home. The servants bring a robe, sandals and a ring to put on the younger son. The father, the younger son and the servants celebrate. Meanwhile, to one side, the elder son is in the field digging with a spade. He hears the celebrations and rushes home, angrily complaining. The father reassures the elder son as the narrator ends the story with verses 31 and 32.

Freeze the scene. Ask each of the characters involved how they felt about playing the part. Likewise, ask the children observing the drama which of the characters they most identified with in the story—the younger son, the elder son, the partygoers, the pigs and so on—and why.

Ask the children what they think the spiritual truth is behind the parable. Encourage them to see that it is about the temptation we all face to live life without God. But Christians believe that God is like a loving father and will always welcome us with open arms if we turn to him. Ask the children to think of the temptations they face day by day.

Ask the children to talk about times when they have managed to rebuild a friendship after falling out with someone.

Reiterate that God is like a loving father who will always welcome us back if we turn to him, but that we also need to say 'sorry' for the things we have thought, said or done that are wrong. We must then try not to do those things again.

Prayer

Light the candle before saying the prayer.

Dear God, we thank you that you are like a loving father and that you welcome us with open arms whenever we say 'sorry' to you for the things we have thought, said or done that are wrong. We ask that you will help us day by day to resist the temptations we face, so that we might walk more closely with you all the days of our life. Amen

Dismissal

Leader: We go knowing God's love and forgiveness.
Response: Thanks be to God.

Suggested music to exit

❂ The Journey of Life (CFW 210)

Optional extras

1 Use a dramatized version of the Bible to tell the parable of the lost son. Get individual characters to learn their lines rather than miming to a narrator.
2 Ask children to go back to their classroom and write a modern-day version of the parable of the lost son (or daughter), focusing on different temptations.

Assembly Two: God's love, forgiveness and re-creation

The following outline is intended to enable the children to appreciate not only God's act of creation but also his continuing involvement in the world. They will be encouraged to see that, whatever people do wrong, God does not give up on us. This is the story of re-creation, of the pivotal significance of Jesus, the growth of the Church and the part we play. The children will be encouraged to see that they, too, can be part of re-creation and that they, too, can make a difference in God's world.

You will need:
✢ A table with cloth and a candle.
✢ A large lump of playdough (ideally about 20cm in diameter). It can be coloured blue to represent the colour of the earth as seen from outer space, or red as a colour of love.
✢ An image of the world taken from outer space (www.nasaimages.org).

To make playdough, mix three cups of plain flour with one and a half cups of salt, three cups of water (with added colouring), three tablespoons of cooking oil and six teaspoons of cream of tartar. Put all the ingredients into a saucepan and stir while cooking gently over a medium heat until the dough is smooth and pliable.

Suggested opening music and entrance

❂ A recording of 'He's got the whole world in his hands' sung by Laurie London

As children enter, have the image of the world showing on the screen.

Christian greeting

Leader: Praise the Lord for he is good.
Response: He will never give up on us. His love will last for ever.

Introduction

Explain to the children that you are going to take them on a journey from the moment God created the world to the present day. Emphasize that Christians believe that, whatever mistakes people make, God never abandons his world and that he offers love, forgiveness and a fresh start to each one of us.

Suggested songs

The King of Love my shepherd is (HON 584)
I am a new creation (HON 221)

Application

Shape the playdough into a globe shape and talk about God creating his world. Mention how Christians believe that the world was good in God's sight (Genesis 1). Shape the dough into a heart to remind the children that God's creation is an act of love. Restore the globe shape.

Next, talk about the story of Adam and Eve and how this speaks of human disobedience and separation from God (Genesis 3). *(Break pieces off the playdough globe to signify God's broken world)* Go on to explain that people have always been capable of spoiling God's creation. *(Break more pieces off the playdough globe)* Remind the children that Christians believe that God never gives up. Talk about God's covenant with Noah, which helped to restore his world. *(Add some broken bits back on to the playdough world)*

Furthermore, through Moses, God gave people ten best ways to help them live in the right way. God promised that if people turned to him and followed his ways, he would be their God. *(Add broken pieces to globe)* Moreover, in response to their continuous disobedience he sent his prophets to call people back to his ways, such as Isaiah, Jeremiah and Ezekiel. Many people responded *(add more broken bits back on to the playdough world)*, but others continued to forget about God. There were wars and rumours of wars, greed, broken relationships and injustice. *(Break more pieces off the playdough world)*

Still God did not give up, and the Bible tells us that he became a human being in the person of Jesus to show people who God was. *(Put more broken pieces back on playdough world)* Christians call Jesus' birth the 'incarnation'. Talk about Jesus' life and about his teaching and healing. Mention the disciples and others who responded to his message. *(Add more broken pieces)*

However, many people—including one of his closest friends, Judas—opposed Jesus, and this led to his death. *(Break big lump off the playdough world)* In the years after Jesus' death and resurrection, his followers continued to teach that Jesus was the Son of God, and the Christian Church was born. Talk about Paul's missionary journeys *(add broken pieces)*. Talk about people who have followed Jesus down the ages *(add broken pieces)*.

Constantly, through the course of history, there have been others who have turned their back on God's ways, and have shown hostility, greed, selfishness and so on. *(Break pieces off the playdough world)* This brings us to today. God still loves his world, but it is in many ways far removed from his original creation. Talk to the children about what we can do to rebuild God's world—for example, being kind to one another—to emphasize that we can each play our part. Invite children to suggest things we can do and, as they do so, reconnect the broken pieces of dough so that God's world is rebuilt.

Once the playdough world is complete again, reshape it into a heart. Remind the children how Christians believe that God created the world out of love, and that, for Christians, our response to him, day by day, is a response of love that rebuilds his world. Remind them that when we make mistakes we can turn to God, say 'sorry', be forgiven and have a fresh start. This is re-creation.

End with an intact world-shaped globe and place it on the table. Light the candle next to the globe.

Prayer

Dear God, we thank you for your wonderful world that you created out of love, and for never giving up on us, even when we turn away from you. Help us to resist the temptations that we face day by day, but when we make mistakes help us always to be prepared to say 'sorry'. Then please forgive us and give us a fresh start. Thank you especially for your Son, Jesus, who showed us the way to be at one with you again. Amen

Dismissal

Leader: Praise the Lord for he is good.
Response: His goodness will last for ever.

Suggested music to exit

✪ 'What a wonderful world' by Louis Armstrong or a song with a similar theme.

Optional extras

1   As the playdough pieces are broken off, use a series of images to illustrate the ways in which people spoil God's creation. Likewise, use images to reflect re-creation as the playdough pieces are reattached to the world.
2   Talk about times when the children have felt recreated, such as when a broken relationship has been restored.

The story of baptism

Key focus: the Holy Spirit who gives life
to the people of God

Background information for the teacher

Just before Jesus' ascension to heaven, he gathered his disciples around him and commissioned them to 'go to the people of all nations and make them my disciples. Baptize them in the name of the Father, and the Son, and the Holy Spirit' (Matthew 28:19). The disciples were, of course, familiar with the practice of baptizing with water, for it had a long history. What was new here was the command to baptize in the name of the Trinity.

Baptism in the New Testament begins with John the Baptist. John baptized people as a sign that they would give up their sins and turn to God (Matthew 3:11). However, it is clear that John expected someone to supersede him who would baptize not just with water, but also with the Holy Spirit and with fire, for the baptism of John did not confer the Spirit (Acts 1:5; 11:15–16; 19:1–6). Jesus was that expected person. In the baptism of Jesus by John, we see the anointing of Jesus as the Messiah.

What seems clear is that, in the early Church, to be 'baptized in the name of Jesus Christ' became an expectation for believers (Acts 2:38) and that this baptism was linked to receiving the gift of the Holy Spirit. The New Testament does not provide us with an exact rite of baptism. Over the centuries that followed, the rite of baptism became more clearly defined and formulated. Thus Tertullian, in the third century, describes a threefold baptism (that is, in the name of the Father, Son and Holy Spirit) by full immersion. After the immersion, those who had been baptized were anointed with oil. There then followed the laying on of hands, during which the gift of the Holy Spirit was given.

The current baptismal rites found in the major Christian churches have a clearly developed structure. In the Anglican tradition, the candidates for baptism (or their parents and godparents) are expected to declare publicly that they renounce the devil and all evil and firmly desire to follow Jesus. They then receive the sign of the cross on their forehead. The water is blessed, but before the baptism the candidates have to make a profession of faith. The baptism follows in the name of the Father, Son and Holy Spirit. The candidates are prayed for, welcomed into the local congregation and sent out with a lighted candle (symbolizing the fact that they have received the light of Christ) and are called to walk in this light for the rest of their lives.

The significance of the Trinity in the Anglican baptismal rite is perhaps most clearly expressed in the 'Prayer over the Water', which can be found at www.cofe.anglican.org (search the website for "holy baptism").

Exploring the story

The word 'baptism' comes from the Greek word *baptismo* meaning 'to dip' or 'immerse'. The Jews practised baptism long before Christianity was born. It had been a common practice to baptize non-Jews (Gentiles) who wished to change direction and become Jews.

John the Baptist was Jesus' cousin, the son of Elizabeth and Zechariah (Luke 1:5–25). John began to make the Jewish authorities angry because he challenged members of the Jewish community to repent and be baptized.

John the Baptist is regarded by Christians as the last of God's messengers preparing the way for the coming of Jesus. Matthew 3:4 tells us that John was dressed in camel hair and wore a leather strap as a belt. He also lived on grasshoppers and wild honey. In verse 13 we are told how John asked Jesus to baptize him.

The story of the baptism of Jesus is found in all four Gospels: Matthew 3:13–17; Mark 1:9–11; Luke 3:21–22 and John 1:29–34. Read each account. You will see that each one talks about the Holy Spirit descending on Jesus like a dove.

Introductory questions about the story

Why was Jesus' baptism such an important event in his life? What is each Gospel trying to say about Jesus through this story?

Introductory tasks

- ❂ Using all four Gospels, imagine that you were present at this event. Write a newspaper report to record the event.
- ❂ Imagine you are John the Baptist. Write the conversation that you would have had with a close friend after this event, explaining the difference between you and Jesus.
- ❂ Design a stained-glass window to depict the event and represent the Trinity.
- ❂ Find out how different denominations throughout the world practise baptism.

Key symbols in the story

The dove

The dove is a Christian symbol of the Holy Spirit.

Water

For Christians, the use of water is important: it cleanses and it is the source of life. Another important significance of water for Christians is that Jesus described himself as 'life-giving water' (John 4:9–15; 7:38).

John's clothes

The Bible says that John wore camel hair and a leather belt. This was the traditional dress for people who followed Asceticism, a life characterized by abstinence. Those who practise ascetic lifestyles often find that this is a good way for them to deepen their spirituality and so grow closer to God.

Understanding the story through the senses

Sight

One of the most famous paintings of the baptism of Jesus is by the Italian artist Piero della Francesca (*Baptism of Christ*), which is now held in the National Gallery in London. This can be found on the website www.nationalgallery.org.uk.

If you look closely at the picture, you will see John baptizing Jesus and the dove hovering above Jesus' head. To the left of Jesus you can see three angels, which represent the Christian concept of Trinity. The angel in red represents God the Father, the angel in blue represents Jesus and the angel in white represents the Holy Spirit. Piero has included the angels to remind us of the three angels that appeared to Abraham in Genesis 18:1–3. If you look carefully, you will see that the angel in blue is divided by a tree trunk. The tree is a walnut tree, which is a symbol of Christ. The first angel's red robe is symbolic of the robe at the crucifixion.

Piero has also painted in the group of Pharisees from Matthew's Gospel, and one other person waiting to be baptized. Although there is only one person, he is painted bending over to symbolize the weight of sin from which he is about to be released.

One of the most interesting features of this painting is the mathematics. It is possible to draw a triangle from John's hand down to the bottom of the painting and from the bottom of Jesus' foot up to the arch above. Framed within these two triangles is the figure of Jesus. A triangle was a key symbol of the Trinity with its three sides.

Cardinal Noccolo Cusano, for whom Piero was working at the time of this painting, was known to have said, 'Since we can only accede to divine things through symbol, we shall use mathematical signs which are an incontrovertible certainty.'

Sound

The Gospel writers talk about the voice of God saying, 'This is my own dear Son, and I am pleased with him.' Read the words of the hymn 'Holy, holy, holy' (HON 210), based on the Trinity. Consider how you could change the words or add a verse to reflect the baptism of Jesus. You might think about the noise of the crowd or the sound of the water splashing.

Smell

The Jordan river was once full of fish. Species such as carp and rainbow trout inhabited the waters. There would also have been various forms of plant life both in the water and on the banks of the river. These would have been the smells of the day on the riverbank.

Touch

A key sense in the process of baptism is touch—for example, the feel of the cool water washing over the body. Think how you might feel on a hot day when you are able to take a cool shower.

Taste

Water, while being refreshing, is relatively tasteless. Nonetheless, those who believed in Jesus and were baptized came to see in him a source of life-giving water (John 4:9–15). They tasted this living water and found that it was good. They would also have remembered the words of Psalm 119:103: 'Your teachings are sweeter than honey.'

A focus table of reflection for the classroom

This table should remind the pupils of the significance of the Trinity. Place three candles on the table in a triangle shape, or find a candle with three wicks. Do not light the candles. Ask the children to think about the unlit candles. What do they look like? Do they appear strange? Place a copy of the Apostles' Creed on the table (this can be found on the Internet using a web search engine), together with an image of Jesus' baptism, a bowl of water and some paper towels.

Explain that the word 'creed' comes from the Latin word *credo* ('I believe'). The creed sets out what Christians believe.

Explain that Christians say the creed together and pray to God the Father, the Son and Holy Spirit.

Next, light the three candles: one for God the Father, one for Jesus the Son and one for the Holy Spirit. Talk about Jesus saying that he was the light for the world. Christians believe that Jesus is like a light entering the darkness of the world.

Ask the children to think about things they might do to become beacons of light in the world. Write down some of the pupils' ideas and place the words on the table.

Show the pupils an image of Jesus' baptism. Talk about how water is used in baptism to show that people want to turn to God and be forgiven for the things they do wrong.

Explain that baptism is about cleansing and refreshing. Invite the children to wash their hands in the bowl of water as a reminder of the Christian belief that God wants to forgive, cleanse and refresh us so that we are ready to begin again.

Reflecting on the story

Assembly One: The service of holy baptism

The following outline, which is based on the Anglican tradition, will help pupils to understand the structure of the baptism service. They will also learn about the significance of the symbolism used and the trinitarian nature of the rite. This is an ideal opportunity to ask your local minister to lead the worship so that the children can experience the current practice in their local church and also see the clothes that a minister would wear, such as robes and the baptismal stole. The example is based on infant baptism but it is important to point out that people may be baptized at any age.

You will need:
+ A bowl to function as a font.
+ A large jug of water.
+ Olive oil.
+ A paschal candle, borrowed from a local church. (The symbolism of this candle can be found in the section on Easter, p. 115.)

✣ A doll to represent the baptism 'candidate'.

✣ A candle to give to the baptism 'candidate'.

✣ Children to take on the roles of parents and godparents. Traditionally there are two godmothers and one godfather for a girl, and two godfathers and one godmother for a boy. Ask the children to dress smartly to signify that this is a special celebration.

✣ An image of the baptism of Jesus, such as Piero della Francesca's *Baptism of Christ*.

✣ A copy of the baptism service, borrowed from a local church.

Suggested opening music and entrance

❂ A recording of 'Have you heard the raindrops?' (*Just Instrumental Hymns and Songs for Children 1*, Kevin Mayhew, 2003)

Project the chosen image on to a screen.

Christian greeting

Leader: Let us give thanks to God: Father, Son and Holy Spirit.
Response: For he longs to give us new life.

Introduction

Refer to the image on the screen and read an account of Jesus' baptism from one of the Gospels (such as Mark 1:9–12). Emphasize the significance of this moment for Jesus as a starting point for his work of teaching people about God. Refer to the dove hovering over Jesus, which signifies God empowering him with the Holy Spirit in preparation for his work.

Now read Matthew 28:16–20, in which Jesus instructs his

disciples to go to the people of all nations and make them his disciples, baptizing them in the name of the Father, the Son and the Holy Spirit. Explain to the children that they are now going to see what happens in a baptism in an Anglican church today.

Suggested song

Sing the following song while you reflect on the chosen image on the screen:

❂ Spirit of the living God, fall afresh on me (HON 454)

Application

Light the paschal candle, reminding the children that this represents the Christian belief that Jesus is the light for the world. Invite the chosen 'parents' and 'godparents' to come forward. Now enact the baptism service, explaining what is happening at each stage:

❂ The decision: the parents and godparents are asked to turn their backs on evil and turn to Christ instead.
❂ Make the sign of the cross with olive oil on the forehead of the 'baby'. Explain the use of holy oil for anointing. (This also happens at a coronation.)
❂ Pour the water from the jug into the 'font'. Refer to water as being the source of life, as the means of washing, cleaning and so on.
❂ The blessing of the water: refer to the prayer in the baptism service.
❂ The 'profession of faith'. Explain that at this point everyone is asked to profess their faith by responding to three questions based on the Trinity:
  • Do you believe and trust in God the Father?
  • Do you believe and trust in his Son, Jesus Christ?
  • Do you believe and trust in the Holy Spirit?

- Pretend to baptize the 'baby'. Pour water over the head of the 'baby' in the name of the Father, Son and Holy Spirit.
- The minister then reminds everyone of their duty to help the child grow in the Christian faith (the so-called 'commission'). This is followed by prayers for the parents and a challenge to everyone present to remain faithful to the candidate's baptism.
- The welcome: this is the moment when the congregation welcomes the newly baptized person. If possible, use the following words from the service on an OHP:

  Minister: There is one Lord, one faith, one baptism. *[Name]*, by one spirit we are all baptized into one body.

  Response: We welcome you into the fellowship of faith; we are children of the same heavenly Father. We welcome you.

- Everyone could share the peace by shaking hands with their closest neighbours and exchanging the words 'The peace of the Lord be with you', to which the response is given, 'And also with you.'
- The 'sending out'. Explain that at this point the priest gives a blessing and the child receives a baptism candle. This is a good moment to explain the significance of the lighted candle (see page 47). Light the baptism candle from the paschal candle and hand it to a parent or godparent to hold for the 'child'.

Prayer

Dear God, by the power of your Holy Spirit you give us new life in the water of baptism. Guide and strengthen us by the same Spirit, that we may serve you faithfully all the days of our life. Amen

Dismissal

Leader: Go in the light of Christ.
Response: Thanks be to God.

Suggested music to exit

The baptism party leads everyone else out, following the baptism candle. Suitable music to exit would again be a recording of 'Have you heard the raindrops?'

Optional extras

1 Arrange for some of the children to design and make a baptism stole for the minister to wear. Explain the symbolism on the stole.
2 Instead of acting out a baptism using a doll, it might be possible for the school community to gather for the actual baptism of one of the school children. Close liaison with the local minister and family is needed here, but the event could be inspirational.

Assembly Two: The Trinity

The following act of worship will help the children to come to an understanding of the Trinity.

You will need:
- ❖ Various props to demonstrate the Trinity, such as a triangle, or a tricycle.
- ❖ A large orange ball to represent the sun.
- ❖ Large card labelled 'heat' and another labelled 'light'.
- ❖ A tube of toothpaste with three coloured stripes.
- ❖ Three hats that a single person might wear: for example, sailor, chef or fire fighter.
- ❖ A jug of water, a bag of ice cubes, and a kettle with water ready to boil.
- ❖ A table with a green tablecloth and three candles.

Suggested opening music and entrance

✪ A recording of 'Holy, holy, holy, Lord God Almighty'

Christian greeting

Leader: Come let us worship the Lord our God.
Response: Father, Son and Holy Spirit.

Introduction

As a backdrop, tell the children about Christopher Columbus' discovery of Trinidad, on his third voyage in 1598. Explain that Columbus was a devout Christian and, whenever he set off on his travels or whenever he wrote a letter, he always began with the words 'In the name of the most Holy Trinity'. Indeed, when he presented his theory of the New World to be discovered, he began, 'I come before you in the name of the most Holy Trinity, because our sovereigns have commanded me to submit to your wisdom a project which has certainly come to me inspired by the same Holy Spirit.' Columbus clearly had a tremendous devotion to the Trinity. So he set out on his third voyage in 1598 and vowed to consecrate to the Trinity the first land that he would discover. Hence the island he reached first was called Trinidad, after the Trinity.

Understanding God as Father, Son and Holy Spirit can prove difficult. Nevertheless, a number of images have been used to help us understand how you can have three persons in one God. We shall now explore some of these images.

Suggested song

Father, we love you (HON 126)

Application

Explain that the word 'Trinity' comes from tri-unity, which means three things united. Show the children a triangle or a tricycle as examples. Ask them to suggest others (such as triathlon, tripod, triptych and so on).

Then explain other images that might be helpful. For example:

⊙ Ask a child to hold the orange ball to represent the sun. Ask another child to hold up the label 'heat', and another the label 'light'. Explain that you can't have one without the other. The three go together.

⊙ Show a tube of toothpaste with three coloured stripes coming out as one.

⊙ Explain that you went to a friend's house and in the hallway, on the hat stand you saw a sailor's hat, a chef's hat and a fire fighter's helmet. Ask for a volunteer. Put the sailor's hat on your volunteer. Explain that the hat belongs to a sailor and he wears this hat when he is on parade. Then replace the sailor's hat with the chef's. Explain that the sailor is the ship's chef and he wears this hat when he is cooking. Then replace the chef's hat with the fire fighter's helmet. Explain that when the sailor is off duty he is a volunteer fire fighter in his local town. So, he is really three people in one: a sailor, a chef and a fire fighter.

⊙ Pour yourself a glass of water and have a drink. Explain that the water is a liquid. Now show the children a bag of ice cubes. Remind them that this is still water but in a solid form. Now boil the kettle so that the children can see the steam. Explain that steam is still water but in a vaporized form. So water can exist in three quite distinct forms—liquid, solid or vapour—but they are all H_2O.

Having revealed these examples, explain that Christians believe that God is also three in one: God the Father, God the Son and God the Holy Spirit. God the Father created the world; God the Son became a human being to show us what God is like. Finally, God the Holy Spirit was with God from the very beginning of creation and is given as our helper when we believe in Jesus. So God exists as three in one—Father, Son and Holy Spirit—the Trinity.

Prayer

Light the three candles. Ask the pupils to reflect on the light. There are three candle flames, but do they make three lights or one?

Pray or sing the following prayer together. It can be sung as a round.

Praise God from whom all blessings flow; praise him, all creatures here below; praise him above, ye heavenly hosts; praise Father, Son and Holy Ghost.

Dismissal

Leader: Go with the love of God.
Response: Father, Son and Holy Spirit; three in one!

Suggested music to exit

Exit to a recording of 'Holy, Holy, Holy, Lord God Almighty'.

Optional extras

1 Instead of ice, water and steam, you could use illustrations of stream, river and sea as being all water.
2 Instead of the illustration of one person as sailor, chef and fire fighter, you could choose the example of someone being a mother, daughter and wife at the same time, making them three in one.

What God has done:
The concept of salvation

This section of the book, which focuses on the concept of salvation, covers the birth of Jesus, his death and resurrection, and the sending of the Holy Spirit at Pentecost.

The word 'salvation' refers to God's act of rescuing his people from slavery or from their enemies. In the Old Testament, God freed the Israelites from slavery in Egypt (Exodus 12:31—14:31) and later continued to free them from their enemies through his kings, warriors or other national leaders. In the higher sense, salvation was always attributed to God.

In the New Testament, God acts to save his people not just from earthly bondage or enemies but also from eternal peril, by sending his Son Jesus into the world. The birth of Jesus, which we celebrate at Christmas, represents a pivotal moment in God's work of salvation. The events of Jesus' life, and especially his death and resurrection, help us to understand how this great act of salvation was achieved.

For Christians, the festival of Pentecost has its rightful place in this work of salvation because the Holy Spirit is the means by which God's purpose is communicated and implemented in the world (Galatians 4:4–6). It is also by the power of the Holy Spirit that the benefits of salvation are received and individuals become more like Christ (Romans 8:5).

God's saving act is probably best summed up in one verse: 'God loved the people of this world so much that he gave his only Son, so that everyone who has faith in him will have eternal life and never really die' (John 3:16).

A good image to use to explore the concept of salvation is *The Trinity* by Masaccio, which can be found by using an Internet search engine.

The story of incarnation

Background information for the teacher

The twelve days of Christmas begin on Christmas Day and end with the feast of the Epiphany on 6 January. The major parts of what we understand to be the Christmas story are to be found in the Gospels of Matthew (chapters 1 and 2) and Luke (chapters 1 and 2). In contrast, there is no reference to the birth of Jesus in either Mark's or John's Gospels, although John does refer to Jesus as a light entering a world of darkness.

Matthew begins his account of the Christmas story with Joseph. Having discovered that Mary, to whom he is engaged, is expecting a baby, Joseph decides not to go ahead with the marriage. However, an angel visits Joseph and explains that he shouldn't be afraid to marry Mary because the child is God's own Son. The story goes on to tell how Joseph did as the angel said and named the child 'Jesus', which means 'one who saves'.

In Luke 1:26–38 we are also told of a visit from an angel. This time it is the angel Gabriel who visits Mary to tell her that God is pleased with her and that she is to have a child, whom she must call Jesus. Christians call the angel's visit to Mary 'the annunciation'. Luke tells how Mary, having heard this message from the angel, sets off to visit her cousin Elizabeth, who is also expecting a baby. Elizabeth's baby is to be John the Baptist. Mary is so happy that she sings a song of praise to God. Her song is known as the Magnificat and can be found in Luke 1:46–55.

It is also in Luke (2:1–20) that we find details of Mary and Joseph's journey to Bethlehem and the birth of Jesus. At the time, the Roman emperor (Augustus) has ordered a census to be taken. Joseph has to return to his family home town of Bethlehem to be registered with Mary. Although, like Matthew, Luke is keen to show that Jesus was descended from the great Old Testament king, David, Luke tells us that Jesus was born in an animal shelter rather than a palace and was visited by shepherds rather than wealthy people from important or royal families. Luke is eager to show that Jesus' birth was for everyone and not just for a privileged few. Christians call Jesus' birth 'the incarnation' because, in Jesus, God became a human being.

The angels in Luke's Gospel tell the shepherds that Jesus is the long-awaited Messiah (God's chosen king, who would rescue his people). However, they will find baby Jesus wrapped in cloth and lying in a manger. This was not the traditional Jewish perception of the Messiah. Luke expresses the simplicity of Jesus' birth as opposed to the Jewish expectation of a kingly, powerful Messiah, born in a royal setting.

Matthew 2:1–12 tells the story of wise men who journey to Bethlehem to worship Jesus. Christians call this part of the story the Epiphany, which means 'showing forth'. The wise men, who are also known as the magi, are the first to show that Jesus has come for all people and not just for people of Jewish birth.

In the first two chapters of Matthew and Luke, we can see that the traditional Christmas story is an amalgamation of the stories in these two Gospels.

Throughout history, colours have been given special meanings. For example, red symbolizes love, and purple symbolizes wisdom. So, too, the church has used different colours for its robes and furnishings to reflect the seasons, special festivals and services. These are called 'liturgical colours'. The liturgical colours for Christmas and Epiphany are white and gold.

Exploring the story

Read the different accounts of the Christmas story in Matthew and Luke and find out which parts of the story and which characters appear in each Gospel. You will see that Luke begins his account with the story of the priest Zechariah and his wife Elizabeth. The angel Gabriel tells Zechariah that Elizabeth will have a son, whom they are to call John. This is the birth account of John the Baptist. The story then goes on to tell of Gabriel's visit to Mary, Jesus' birth in Bethlehem and the visit of the shepherds. Matthew, however, focuses on the stories surrounding Joseph and the journey of the wise men.

The explorer Marco Polo was given a version of an old Persian legend about the wise men, on his way to the court of Kublai Khan in the 13th century. According to the legend, based on the story in the Gospel, three kings named Caspar, Melchior and Balthasar saw a bright star on the night Christ was born and followed it to Bethlehem. There they found the child and offered the gifts of gold, frankincense and myrrh. Read the story again in Matthew. How many wise men are there in Matthew's Gospel?

Introductory questions about the story

- ☉ Would Jesus be born to a single parent today? If not, what would be the circumstances of his parents?
- ☉ If Jesus was born today, who might visit him?
- ☉ Reflect on what you might take as a gift to the baby Jesus.

Introductory tasks

- Using a selection of religious Christmas cards, decide which Gospel the artist used for his or her inspiration.
- Repeat this task, but use Christmas carols instead of Christmas cards.
- Write a diary account, as if you were either Mary or Joseph, explaining the events of the nativity from your perspective.
- Find out how other countries celebrate Christmas and Epiphany.

Key symbols in the story

Bethlehem

Both Matthew and Luke agree that the birthplace of Jesus was Bethlehem. This is an important fulfilment of the Old Testament prophecies and establishes Jesus as the successor to King David, who was also thought to have been born in Bethlehem (see 1 Samuel 16:1; Micah 5:2).

The star

The tradition of the star appearing as a heavenly sign at the time of Jesus' birth was seen by Matthew as a fulfilment of Old Testament prophecy: 'Some day, a king of Israel will appear like a star' (Numbers 24:17) and 'Nations and kings will come to the light of your dawning day' (Isaiah 60:3).

The stable

The stable expresses the simplicity of Jesus' birth in a place traditionally used by animals, as opposed to the Jewish perception of the Messiah and ideas about how this powerful king would be born.

The Advent ring

The first candle of the ring is lit on Advent Sunday, and an additional one is lit on each of the following Sundays. The candles represent the patriarchs, the prophets, John the Baptist and the Virgin Mary. Finally, the central candle is lit on Christmas Day to symbolize Jesus as the light for the world (John 1:8–9; 8:12). You will note that, for Christians, the Advent ring summarizes the events leading up to the birth of Jesus.

Angels

Angels are traditionally regarded as God's messengers and, in the nativity story, they appear to both the shepherds in Luke's account and the wise men in Matthew's. The word 'angel' comes from the Greek word *angelos*. In Persian, *angaros* means 'courier', in Hebrew the word is *mal'akh*, meaning 'ambassador', and in Sanskrit it is *angiras*, meaning 'divine spirit'.

Gold, frankincense and myrrh

Matthew's account of the wise men visiting Jesus as a very young child is of particular interest as the symbols of gold, frankincense and myrrh tell us something about the life and death of Jesus.

- Gold symbolizes kingship. Although it is a precious and noble metal that does not corrode, at the time of the birth of Jesus gold was less precious than frankincense.
- Frankincense is a natural substance gathered from the Boswellia tree. It was regarded as precious and was used in worship in great quantities. Frankincense was used to embalm corpses but it was also said to have rejuvenating properties with its flesh-preserving

qualities. The word 'frank' means 'pure' and refers to the pure gum. The substance becomes 'incense' when perfumes and spices are added. Both natural frankincense and incense have been burned for centuries for purification purposes. It is also said that, during the Black Death in England, the perfumers and embalmers who burned frankincense did not die from the diseases of their patients.

❂ Myrrh also comes from a gum resin, which originated in Arabia and Persia and has been used in religious ceremonies since antiquity. The ancient Egyptians called it *phun* and it was used for embalming. Myrrh has good antiseptic qualities and reduces inflammation. Today it is often used to treat acne and dermatitis.

Understanding the story through the senses

Sight

Use an image of the painting by Stefano da Zevio entitled *Adoration of the Magi*. This can be found on the Internet using a web search engine.

What can you see in the painting? Compare the way the artist has painted the picture with the Gospel account. Is it an accurate picture of the Gospel stories? Which Gospel has the artist used to enhance and develop the story?

Who are the other characters in the painting? What are they doing? Why do you think the artist has put them all in? Are they all necessary to the story? The older woman behind Mary is thought to represent St Ann, Mary's own mother.

If you look top left of the painting, you will see that the shepherds have left the scene and are returning to their flocks in the hills. If you look closely, you will see that there is a wolf in the top right-hand corner of the picture. There are several references to wolves in the Bible. They usually represent something that is vicious, fearsome and ravenous, poised to attack the innocent sheep. Here we have an innocent child, but the wolf is lurking in the background. Jesus, the 'Lamb of God' as he is known, is thus depicted with echoes of the shadow of death waiting in the darkness.

The wise men (magi) are offering their gifts of gold, frankincense and myrrh. It is worth pointing out that in Northern European paintings the containers for these gifts gradually became more precious as promotional images and advertising for the local goldsmiths.

One of the wise men has taken off his crown as a symbol of homage to the child Jesus. Think about the symbolism of the gifts. What do they foretell?

Sometimes, in paintings of the Epiphany, Mary appears to be holding the baby Jesus back from the gifts, protecting him from what is to be his fate. In this painting, however, Mary really is 'showing forth' the baby, who appears to be receiving the gifts. Mary is looking very pensive. Why do you think this is?

There are also lots of animals in the picture, including a dog, which appears to be chewing an animal that has just been hunted. Traditionally, this idea was also linked to Jesus' death. There is also a peacock perched on top of the stable roof to symbolize the kingship of Jesus. Traditionally, peacocks were found in royal gardens.

Sound

Listen to some music based on the Christmas story—for example, 'Once in royal David's city', 'O little town of Bethlehem', 'While shepherds watched their flocks by night', or 'We three kings of Orient are'. There are many popular CDs containing Christmas carols and music.

Reflect on the words and think about which composer has best captured the Gospel story. Consider some of the sounds that might have been heard in the stable when Jesus was born. Reflect on the sound of a newborn baby. Would Jesus have been any different?

Smell

Using various examples of incense, frankincense and myrrh, explore the smells involved in the story. Burn some incense or incense sticks to see how the smoke pervades the atmosphere. Consider what other smells might have been present at the nativity scene.

Touch

Look closely at paintings or Christmas cards of the Epiphany. Consider the ways in which Mary is holding the baby. Is she holding the baby in a way that 'shows him forth' to the wise men?

Taste

Mince pies are popular at Christmas but we often forget that originally they were baked to represent the crib. Traditionally, there was a marzipan baby inside and the top represented the cover. In Victorian times, it was felt inappropriate to bite off the head of the Christ-child, so the pie was covered completely and the baby removed. The mince-meat inside represents the spices given by the wise men.

Find out about Epiphany cakes and tarts. They are a special part of the celebrations in some parts of Europe. You might like to make one and taste it. Recipes can be found on the Internet.

A focus table of reflection for the classroom

In most churches the wise men are not placed into the crib scene until the feast of Epiphany on 6 January. It is then the tradition in many churches that the crib scene with the wise men remains in place until the feast of Candlemas on 2 February. Candlemas celebrates the presentation of the eight-day-old Jesus in the temple (Luke 2:25–33).

Schools may like to keep these 40 days special in the following way:

❂ Have a special table with a crib scene. The liturgical colour is white or gold. During each of the 40 days, remove one of the animals and characters, shepherds, wise men, angels and so on until Candlemas, when only the holy family remains (Mary, Joseph and the baby Jesus). Star shapes or stars stuck on to prayer beads or pebbles might be used for pupils' individual prayers and reflections.

You might like to read the following Candlemas prayer:

Father, here we bring to an end our celebration of the Saviour's birth. Be with us now as we journey towards Easter.

Reflecting on the story

Assembly One: The heart of the nativity

The following outline helps pupils to remember that the most important part of Christmas is the birth of Jesus. It is good to celebrate, to party and to have fun, but we mustn't forget that Christmas is about God's Son being born as a human being (the incarnation).

You will need:
✣ A table with a white or gold cloth and a white candle.
✣ Children and props to make up a traditional nativity scene, together with various other aspects of secular Christmas celebrations. These will include:

- For the traditional nativity: a manger with baby Jesus wrapped in white cloth; pupils dressed as Mary, Joseph, angels, shepherds, wise men (bearing gifts), a donkey, sheep, and cattle.
- For the secular celebrations: the same as for the traditional nativity, plus extra animals such as penguins, dinosaurs and so on; a street trader selling hot chestnuts; a child wrapping a Christmas present; an adult pouring a glass of wine; Father Christmas and reindeer; children partying with party poppers.

Suggested opening music and entrance

❂ Secular Christmas music, such as 'Merry Christmas everybody' by Slade

Christian greeting

In this instance, use a more traditional Christmas greeting, such as the one below.

Leader: Happy Christmas everyone!
Response: Come, let us celebrate!

Introduction

Talk to the children about some of the things we do to celebrate Christmas (include secular as well as religious elements). Explain that they are now going to arrange a living tableau to illustrate these various components of Christmas celebrations.

Suggested songs

Away in a manger (HON 51)
Silent night (HON 444)
O little town of Bethlehem (HON 377)

Application

Construct a living tableau representing scenes of Christmastide. Start with the manger and baby Jesus. Add in sequence Mary, Joseph, a donkey, cattle, angels, shepherds, sheep, and wise men bearing gifts. Then, to the sound of secular Christmas music, bring alongside the street trader, the child wrapping the present, the adult pouring a glass of wine, Father Christmas, reindeer, and a Christmas tree. When these are all in place, add the group of partying children pulling party poppers.

Now stop the music and freeze the scene. Read the account of the nativity story from Luke 2:1–20. Talk to the children about the fun we have at Christmas. Emphasize that there is nothing wrong with this, provided we do not lose sight of what is at the heart of it all.

Next, ask the children what is least important about Christmas. As they respond, 'peel off' those components from the Christmas tableau in front of them. This is an opportunity to remind the children of what the four Gospel writers actually say and do not say about Jesus' birth. The secular components of our Christmas celebration should be removed from the scene in sequence, eventually leaving just the baby in the manger. That is at the heart of the story—God's only Son being born as a tiny baby (the incarnation).

Light the candle on the table and place it behind the manger with the baby. If possible, dim the lights.

Prayer

Dear God, we thank you for all the fun of Christmas—for the laughter, the food, the sounds of partying, the joy of giving and receiving presents and the opportunity to meet with friends and loved ones. But above all we thank you for the love you showed by sending us your Son, Jesus, born in a manger. Help us always to keep Jesus' birth at the heart of Christmas as we enjoy these joyful celebrations. Amen

Dismissal

Leader: Go with the peace of Jesus—the Christ child.
Response: Thanks be to God.

Suggested music to exit

The children leave quietly to the music of a well-known Christmas carol, such as 'Hark! the herald-angels sing'.

Optional extras

1 You could add scenes of celebration from other countries to the tableau: for example, Australians at a barbecue.
2 Construct two separate nativity scenes, one based on Luke's account and the other on Matthew's. Then merge them. This will emphasize the two different Gospel accounts.

Assembly Two: A light for all nations

The following reflection aims to help consolidate the pupils' understanding of the Epiphany story and the significance of the gifts presented to Jesus by the wise men. The reflection also aims to help pupils understand that Epiphany is an important festival around the world.

As part of the reflection, you could dress pupils to represent the wise men. You could also make an Epiphany cake (or cakes) and ask one pupil or member of staff to come forward and receive the cake for their class. The pupils dressed as the wise men would then process down the hall following the star. The pupils (or staff) carrying the cake follow in the procession. The cake is then cut and shared in each class.

You will need:
✢ An image of the Epiphany story.
✢ Gold, frankincense and myrrh.
✢ A table with a white or gold cloth and a candle.
✢ A Bible.
✢ An Epiphany cake.

An Epiphany cake

✢ 300g white flour
✢ 300g sugar
✢ Three tsp baking powder
✢ One tsp salt
✢ 150g margarine
✢ 250ml milk
✢ One and a half tsp vanilla
✢ Two eggs

Preheat oven to 180°C/350°F/Gas Mark 4. Lightly grease and flour two 20cm square cake tins, or one 23cm x 33cm loaf tin. Mix together flour, sugar, baking powder and salt in a large bowl. Drop in the margarine. Pour in 200ml of milk and the vanilla. Mix at a medium speed with an electric mixer until well blended. Add the 50ml of milk and the eggs and beat for two minutes.

If desired, add beans, money or small figures (make sure they are heatproof and suitable for the age of the children). Stir gently. Pour the mixture intò the baking tin(s) and bake for 25 minutes. Cool for ten minutes before turning out on to a cake rack.

Suggested opening music and entrance

❂ A recording of 'We three kings of Orient are'

Christian greeting

Leader: A child has been born for us.
Response: We have been given a son!

Introduction

Recap on the characters in the image. Explore the pupils' knowledge and understanding of where the artist found his or her ideas, and the concept of Epiphany (meaning 'showing forth').

Suggested song

Be still, for the presence of the Lord (HON 53)

Application

Ask three pupils to carry in the gifts of gold, frankincense and myrrh. Explain the significance of the three gifts and place them on the table. Return to the introductory carol and go through the verses in detail—for example, 'Born a king...', 'frankincense', 'myrrh' and so on. Explain how the symbolism of the gifts refers to Jesus' future life and death. Talk about the festival of Epiphany as a celebration of the way in which Jesus is revealed to the world. Link this with the story of Simeon (Luke 2:22–32 and Simeon's statement that Jesus would be 'a light for all nations' (v. 32).

Discuss the idea of light, and the different ways light can guide us through darkness. Explain that Christians believe that, by following

Jesus and his teachings, they have a guiding light to show the way through life. Light the candle.

Prayer

Heavenly Father, we thank you that you used a shining star to guide the wise men to worship Jesus in the stable at Bethlehem. As we share the Epiphany cake, help us to remember that we too can be a small part of that light. Bless our homes and help each one of us in our small way to love one another and make not only our homes but also our world a better place. In this way we can shine for you and be like stars, drawing others to know and worship Jesus.

Dismissal

Leader: Go with the peace of Jesus—the Christ child.
Response: Thanks be to God.

Suggested music to exit

❂ A recording of 'The first Nowell'

Optional extras

1 Go on to talk about how important the festival of Epiphany is in Europe and the ways in which the festival is celebrated in other parts of the world.
2 Discuss ways in which Christians might more effectively tell others about Jesus.

The story of Lent

Background information for the teacher

The English word 'lent' means 'spring'. The season of Lent begins on Ash Wednesday and continues to Easter, a period covering just over six weeks (40 days, plus the Sundays that fall in that period). For Christians, this has become a time of preparation for Easter, when they remember the 40 days and 40 nights that Jesus spent in the desert preparing for his ministry.

For Jesus, this was a time of fasting and, therefore, giving things up (especially luxury food items) has become one activity associated with Lent today. Lent is a time of new beginnings, a time when Christians are able to change their ways and make a fresh start. It is seen as a special time to say 'sorry' to God for wrongdoing, but also to draw closer to God in prayer.

In the early Church, Lent was the time when candidates were prepared for baptism at Easter. For such candidates, it was a time of self-examination, repentance, prayer, fasting and self-denial. For Christians today, the first day of Lent is called Ash Wednesday because of the custom of putting ashes on the heads of believers on that day as a sign of penitence. This custom began in the tenth century, but the use of ashes in this context had a much longer history. Long before Jesus' day, ashes were associated with penitence. The Bible tells us that when the prophet Daniel fasted, he wore sackcloth and sat in ashes while he prayed to God and confessed the sins of his people (Daniel 9:3–4).

It is worth noting that Ash Wednesday marks a stark contrast to the previous day, traditionally known as Shrove Tuesday (the last day before Lent). In many countries Shrove Tuesday is called 'Mardi Gras', or 'Fat Tuesday' and is marked by feasting and carnival in preparation for the 40 days of fasting. Symbolically, it is a time to use up stored rich food in preparation for the austere time to follow. In Britain it is traditional to make pancakes to use up flour and eggs.

Many churches also 'give up' things, such as flower decorations, in an attempt to change the mood and help members of the congregation enter into the experience of this special time. In some churches, parts of the main service may also be omitted, such as some music and singing, or saying joyful 'alleluias'. Vestments and altar frontals are changed to the more sombre colour of purple, deep blue or unbleached white. (The liturgical colour for Lent is purple.) Although it is less common today, some churches cover statues and crosses so that the church is less ornate. This is a 'dressing down' of the church rather than 'dressing up'. It equates to the wearing of sackcloth, rather than fine clothes, as a sign of penitence.

Exploring the story

Read the story of the temptations of Jesus, which is recorded in Matthew 4:1–11, Mark 1:12–13 and Luke 4:1–13. Following his baptism by John, Jesus was led by the Holy Spirit into the desert, where he stayed for 40 days and 40 nights, preparing to begin his work for God. The Judean desert was a very hostile place and, although the Jewish people thought that God's voice could be heard in the quietness of the desert and the mountains, they also thought it was the place where evil spirits and the devil lived. The story tells how, after several days, when Jesus had become very hungry, he was tempted three times by Satan (the devil). The first temptation was to turn stones into bread, thus satisfying Jesus' hunger during his abstinence from food. The second was to throw himself off the top of the temple and have angels to break his fall. Such a miracle would surely impress those who witnessed it. The third temptation was to bow down and worship the devil; for this he would receive all the kingdoms of the world. Jesus resisted these three temptations. His eyes were focused on seeking God's ways, and he would not be deflected in this mission.

Introductory questions about the story

Why do you think Matthew and Luke put such an emphasis on this story compared with Mark and John? What were they trying to say about Jesus?

Introductory tasks

☉ Read the different versions of the story in the Gospels. Find out if they are all the same or how they vary. Make a chart to outline the similarities and differences in the accounts.

☉ Think about the idea of fasting and going without food. Do you think it would be easy? Consider why Christians might go without food for a while. What might it tell them about themselves?

☉ Try to think of a time when you have been tempted to do something wrong. How did it make you feel? How do you feel when you are able to resist temptation?

☉ Using the Internet, find out how Shrove Tuesday and Lent are celebrated and commemorated in other countries. (A key word is 'carnival'.)

Key symbols in the story

The Judean desert

This is the desert area (sometimes known as the wilderness in the Bible) north of Jerusalem. There is practically no water and there is constant fear of starvation. In summer the temperature soars to over 37 degrees Celsius (100 degrees Fahrenheit) every day. As well as the danger from heat and lack of food and water, there is also the danger of roving wild animals and snakes. Although the desert is seen to be an inhospitable place, it was also a place where the Jewish people thought God's voice could be heard. Today Christians use the phrase 'to be in the desert (or wilderness)' to mean feeling lost and alone.

Angels

In the Bible, angels are God's servants and messengers—heavenly beings who spend their time constantly worshipping and serving God. At the end of Jesus' time in the desert, God's angels are described as helping him (Matthew 4:11).

Satan (the devil)

The Bible teaches that some angels rebelled against God and fell from their original sinless state (2 Peter 2:4 and Jude 6). Satan is the leader of these fallen angels, which are seen as being capable of tempting human beings to do wrong. In the story, Jesus is tempted by the devil to do wrong, which illustrates the struggle between good and evil.

Bread and stones

The story tells how Jesus was tempted to turn stones into bread. Jesus was able to resist the temptation even though he was hungry.

The temple in Jerusalem

The temple was the most holy site for the Jewish people and was located on the Temple Mount in the old city of Jerusalem. According to classical Jewish belief, it was the primary resting place of God's presence in the physical world. The first temple was built by King Solomon in the tenth century BC. It was the centre of ancient Judaism and has remained a focal point for Jewish worship over the millennia.

Understanding the story through the senses

Sight

Obtain an image of *Christ in the Wilderness* by Moretto da Brescia (Alessandro Bonvicino). This can be found on the Internet using a web search engine.

If you look closely, you will see Jesus looking pensive with his hand on his chin. It is clearly a time of reflection for Jesus. The artist has painted in some angels but these good angels do not intervene. They are hovering, waiting to attend to Jesus' needs. What do the Gospel writers say about the angels in the story?

Jesus is also surrounded by wild animals, as in Mark's account, when he talks about Jesus being alone with the wild beasts (1:13). How many can you see?

To the left of the painting you will see a stag. This reflects the words in Psalm 42:1 'As a deer gets thirsty for streams of water, I truly am thirsty for you, my God.' In medieval times it was believed that the stag was impervious to snake venom because it drank spring water. The idea of the stag in this painting is that Christians can also resist sin by following Christ and obeying God. The artist has also included an olive tree, which is a powerful reminder for those looking at the painting that it was in the Garden of Olives that Jesus prayed the night before he was crucified.

The sight of people with crosses on their foreheads on Ash Wednesday (the custom of 'ashing') is also a powerful Lenten symbol. For Christians, it is a reminder of the need to repent of wrongdoing, as well as being a reminder of our mortality.

Sound

Listen to the words of the song 'As pants the hart for cooling steams' by Tate and Brady, which is based on Psalm 42. It could be used as a reflection on the painting by Moretto da Brescia.

What sounds might you hear when you are alone? Silence can be very difficult for some people, but a period of silence might help us to listen to our thoughts and think about the sort of person we are. Christians believe that it is easier to hear the voice of God when we are quiet. Think about what this might mean. Think about what other sounds Jesus might have heard in the desert, as well as those of wild animals. How do you think he felt?

Smell

Think about the smell of food, particularly bread. Jesus was hungry. What sort of food do you think he might have reflected on?

Touch

Imagine being alone. How would you feel? Might you be afraid? Touch is an important sense when we are with others. Often, when we are afraid, we find comfort in holding hands. We greet people by shaking hands or kissing. We hold those we love and feel comfortable with. Jesus had no one to touch. It would also have been very hot. The sand, rocks and stones would all have been hot to touch during the day but in the evening the temperature would drop and it might have been quite cold.

The ritual of 'ashing' on Ash Wednesday is a very important sign using the sense of touch. Individuals may feel touched by God.

Taste

Have you ever felt hungry or thirsty? How does it feel? What effect does it have on you physically? How does your mouth feel? Imagine how Jesus felt.

A focus table of reflection for the classroom

On Ash Wednesday, ask the pupils to write down on a piece of paper those things that they would like to improve about their behaviour during Lent, or things that they will attempt to give up. Put a purple tablecloth and candle on a table and place the pieces of paper into a box on the table. Have available a length of thread and 40 beads.

During each of the 40 days, ask one child to come out and light the candle on behalf of all the others, and to place a prayer bead on to the thread. They may like to say a prayer of their own, or perhaps read a prayer such as the one below.

Dear God, by your Holy Spirit, help us to resist the temptations we face day by day. When we fail to do what is right, help us to turn to you for forgiveness, so that we might have a fresh start and be enabled to blossom as children of light. Amen

At the end of the 40 days, explain to the children that many of the world faiths use prayer beads as a focus for prayer. In this activity the children have created their own set.

It might be an idea to keep the days of Lent in mind by using a flipboard with the numbers 1 to 40 written on it. The individual pupils' prayers could be attached to this board. At the end of Lent, the class can reflect on whether or not they have achieved the goals that they placed in the box 40 days earlier. The prayer beads can be displayed as a reminder of those goals.

Reflecting on the story

Assembly One: Dressing up and dressing down

This assembly shows the contrast between Shrove Tuesday and the Lenten season. The following outline aims to help pupils appreciate the contrast between times in our life when we celebrate and dress up (such as for a wedding) and other times when we dress down (such as when we are in mourning). It focuses on the stark contrast between the excitement of Shrove Tuesday and the more sombre, reflective mood of Lent.

You will need:
+ A table with a purple tablecloth and purple candle.
+ Two images: one of a carnival and the other of Jesus' temptations (such as Moretto da Brescia's *Christ in the Wilderness*).
+ Carnival masks (the children could make these in advance).
+ Dressing-up clothes for one person in carnival (a brides-maid's dress would make a good ballgown).
+ Dressing-down clothes, such as a piece of hessian with holes cut for arms and head.
+ Accessories such as make-up to go with dressing up and ash powder to go with dressing down. (Churches make their ash by burning last year's palm crosses, but any fine ash will do.)

Suggested opening music and entrance

⚙ Children enter wearing carnival masks to carnival music, such as Saint-Saens' *Carnival of the Animals*, with an image of a carnival projected on the screen.

Christian greeting

Leader: Be with us now, Lord Jesus.
Response: As we follow in your Lenten footsteps.

Introduction

Talk about the carnival atmosphere of Shrove Tuesday and about how the day is celebrated in other countries. Explain the following facts about Shrove Tuesday and the season of Lent.

⚙ It is a time of preparation for the season of Lent, which begins with Ash Wednesday.
⚙ It is a time to use up stored rich food in preparation for the austere time of fasting that is to follow. (This involves pancake making in Britain, to use up eggs and flour.)
⚙ The name 'Shrove' Tuesday is derived from the word 'shrive', which is about saying sorry to God and receiving forgiveness for past wrongdoings. This becomes a key focus for Lent.
⚙ The traditions of Lent have their roots in the account of Jesus resisting temptation in the desert (read Matthew 4:1–11).
⚙ This is a time of contrasts between dressing up for the celebration of Shrove Tuesday and dressing down for the penitential period of Lent.

Suggested songs

Come on and celebrate (HON 95)
Jubilate, ev'rybody (HON 284)

Let us praise God together (HON 300)
Thank you, Lord, for this fine day (HON 468)

As the song is sung, light the purple candle.

Application

Dress up a child for carnival—for example, with a colourful bolero or long dress, and a mask. Talk about other times in our lives when we dress up to celebrate, such as for a wedding or a birthday party. Talk about other things we do to make ourselves feel special, such as putting on make-up, or having a haircut. Talk about being in a party mood; the mood is joyful, everyone smiles and happiness is all around us. Refer to the carnival image.

Then show the contrast by 'dressing down' a child. Put the sackcloth (hessian tunic) over their clothes. Talk about the times in our lives when we dress down, such as at a funeral, when we wear more sombre colours, fly flags at half mast or play solemn music to express our sadness. Put some ash on the child's forehead. Explain the significance of sackcloth and ashes to Jewish people and the custom of ashing in Christian churches. Biblical examples of ashing can be found in Esther 4:1–3 or Jonah 3:5–9 (where even the animals had to wear sackcloth).

Talk about Lent as a penitential time, when the mood is more reflective than joyful, when Christians think of the temptations they face from day to day and how they seek God's help in resisting them. Talk about how, for Christians, fasting has been valued as a means of focusing on God and seeking his will. Change the projected image from carnival to the painting by Moretto da Brescia.

Prayer

Dear God, we thank you for times of celebration in our lives when we can be joyful and happy. During this season of Lent, we also thank you for the times of reflection, when we can find inspiration to follow Jesus' example and resist temptation. As the Holy Spirit led Jesus, so we pray that he might lead us too. Amen

Dismissal

Leader: Go with hope and joy in your hearts.
Response: Thanks be to God.

Suggested music to exit

❂ A recording of 'Forty days and forty nights'
❂ A recording of 'Father, hear the prayer we offer'

Optional extras

1 Talk about the temptations that we find most difficult to resist in life.
2 Talk about the value of giving things up for Lent and the value of doing the opposite and taking on good things for life.

Assembly Two: Resisting temptation

The following outline aims to help pupils recognize the temptations they face day by day and the life-giving possibilities that exist when temptations are resisted.

You will need:
✤ A table with a purple tablecloth and purple candle.
✤ A large bucket with a bright artificial flower plant in its own pot inside, so that the flower heads just emerge from the bucket.

❖ Image to project, such as Moretto da Brescia's *Christ in the Wilderness*.
❖ A Bible.
❖ A separate empty bucket.
❖ A large jug of water.

Gently surround and cover the plant in the bucket with a number of 10cm pebbles or smooth stones. The flower should be out of sight. Each stone should be labelled, ideally with a water-soluble marker pen, with one of the following words: lying; envy; stealing; hatred; greed; insensitivity; fighting; laziness; jealousy; killing; selfishness; bullying; nastiness; anger; cruelty; racism. Place the filled bucket, containing flower and stones, on the table.

Suggested opening music and entrance

❂ Sing the hymn 'Be still, for the presence of the Lord' (HON 53) Project Moretto da Brescia's image on to a screen.

Christian greeting

Leader: Be with us now, Lord Jesus.
Response: As we follow in your Lenten footsteps.

Introduction

Read Luke 4:1–13. Remind the children that Jesus had just been baptized in the river Jordan and had then been led by the Holy Spirit into the desert. Talk about the three temptations that Jesus experienced over those days, and how he resisted them. Refer to the projected image.

Suggested song

- ✪ Forty days and forty nights
- ✪ Father, hear the prayer we offer (HON 120)

Application

Talk with the children about the temptations we face day by day. Illustrate the talk by asking children to remove one stone at a time from the bucket. As each stone is removed, talk about the particular issue it illustrates. Place each stone into another empty bucket placed at the foot of the table.

As the stones are gradually removed, so the hidden flower inside the bucket will be revealed. When all the stones have been removed, place the flowerpot on the table. Light the candle. Talk about how the stones represent the things we do wrong in life and how, by removing them, we, just like the plant, can be free to grow and blossom.

Remind the children that Christians believe that, like a loving parent, God understands when we sometimes fail to do what is right. By turning to him and saying 'sorry', we can have a fresh start and we will be forgiven.

Prayer

As this prayer is said, pour the water over the stones in the bucket as a reminder that God can wash away all wrongdoing and give us a fresh start.

Dear God, by your Holy Spirit, help us to resist the temptations we face day by day. When we fail to do what is right, help us to turn to you for forgiveness so that we might have a fresh start and be enabled to blossom as children of light. Amen

Suggested closing song

God forgave my sin in Jesus' name (HON 167)
What a friend we have in Jesus (HON 541)
Be still, for the presence of the Lord (HON 53)

Dismissal

Leader: Go with hope and joy in your hearts.
Response: Thanks be to God.

Optional extras

1 Children could each be given a pebble to hold as they reflect on
  the things they do wrong. As they exit, they could drop this
  pebble into a pool of water, not only as a sign of their saying
  'sorry' but also as a sign of God's forgiveness.
2 As a sign of saying 'sorry', each child could tie a 15cm red ribbon
  (or piece of wool) to a 2m-long rope. When each child has tied
  his or her ribbon, the rope could be draped over a large cross as
  an offering to Jesus or simply placed on the purple tablecloth
  with the lighted candle.

The story of Holy Week

Background information for the teacher

Holy Week is the last week of Lent and lasts from Palm Sunday to the Saturday before Easter Day. It is very important for Christians because it covers the final days of Jesus' life, a period known as the passion. The week includes a number of significant events leading up to the burial of Jesus. The first day of Holy Week is Palm Sunday and the account of what happened that day is recorded in each of the four Gospels. Christian churches celebrate Palm Sunday with a re-enactment of Jesus' entry into Jerusalem, involving processions (sometimes with a donkey), the waving of palm branches and shouts of 'Hosanna'.

The Monday of Holy Week recalls the occasion when Jesus went into the temple in Jerusalem and drove out the money changers and all those who were buying and selling goods in the temple courts. The chief priests and teachers of the Law heard about what Jesus had done and began to look for ways to kill Jesus. In the days that followed, Jesus spent much time teaching people about God. The people responded with such enthusiasm that Jesus' opponents became even more determined to eliminate him.

The Thursday of Holy Week is known as Maundy Thursday. This is a special day when Christians remember the day before Jesus died. Events on this day include the last supper, the agony in the garden of Gethsemane and Jesus' arrest. During the last supper, which Jesus shared with his friends, he changed the words of the traditional Passover meal and commanded his followers to break bread and drink wine in his memory. This act of remembrance is known as the Eucharist, Holy Communion, Mass or the Lord's Supper.

Before sharing this Passover meal with the disciples, Jesus washed their feet as a sign of his humility and servanthood. This action is often re-enacted in churches today as part of the celebration of Maundy Thursday. During the last supper, Jesus predicted that one of those present (Judas) would betray him. Judas had already agreed with the chief priests that he would lead them to Jesus in exchange for money, and so he left the room to do just that.

At the end of their meal, Jesus and the other disciples went out to the garden of Gethsemane. There Jesus prayed intensely while the disciples slept. After a short while, Judas arrived with a large crowd armed with swords and clubs, sent by the chief priests. They arrested Jesus but the disciples ran away. Some Christians today remember this last night of Jesus' life with a reflective act of worship called a Gethsemane Watch, which continues until midnight. This is a time for quiet reflection and prayer on the significance of the night.

The following day is called Good Friday and is one of the most holy days in the Christian calendar. It is the day that recalls Jesus' trial, his journey to the cross and his death and burial. In many churches the final hours of Jesus' life are remembered in a service of devotion from 12.00 noon until 3.00 pm, which is the time regarded as the 'ninth hour' when Jesus finally died on the cross. In some communities there is also a procession following a large cross, a public witness by Christians to remind everyone of the significance of this day.

The following day, the last day of Holy Week, is the day when Christians remember Jesus' body lying in the tomb, protected by guards. In church it is also a day of preparation for the celebration of Easter Day, which is to follow. During Holy Week, the Lenten custom of dressing down the church continues, but now, on the Saturday before Easter Day, the community often gathers to 'dress up' the church with bright flowers and so on, ready for Easter Day. On the eve of Easter Day, many churches have a vigil of watching and waiting. This echoes the custom in the early Church of keeping a vigil throughout that night, meditating on the acts of God in scripture and praying until dawn, when the resurrection of Jesus was celebrated. Easter vigil services may also include baptisms and confirmations, a practice which, again, follows the custom of the early Church.

The traditional liturgical colour for the first part of Holy Week is red, but on Maundy Thursday it changes to white. On Good Friday and the Saturday before Easter, it is traditional for altar frontals and other hangings to be removed totally, as a reminder of the barrenness of the tomb.

Exploring the story

The story of Holy Week, known as the passion, is found in each of the four Gospels: Matthew 21:1—27:66, Mark 11:1—15:47; Luke 19:28—23:56 and John 12:12—19:42. The story tells the events of the last week of Jesus' life, the gathering storm of protest against him and, finally, his arrest, trial and crucifixion. The events move from Jesus' being hailed as a king on Palm Sunday, to his being nailed to the cross on Good Friday, with the inscription 'Jesus of Nazareth, King of the Jews' on the cross above his head. Diagram 2 opposite shows the events as they unfold in the four Gospels.

Introductory questions about the story

Read the story of Holy Week in Mark's Gospel. Now compare some of the key events in Mark with another Gospel. Watch a DVD or video of the events in Holy Week. *Jesus of Nazareth* by Franco Zeffirelli is a good example. Compare the film version with one of the Gospels.

Diagram 2	Matthew	Mark	Luke	John
The triumphal entry	21:1–10	11:1–11	19:28–44	12:12–15
Jesus in the temple	21:12–16	11:11–19	19:45–46	
Jesus teaching	21:17—25:46	11:20—14:9	20:1—21:38	12:20–50
The plot and betrayal	26:1–5, 14–16	14:10–11	22:1–6	13:18–30
The last supper	26:17–35	14:12–31	22:7–38	13:1–30
The garden of Gethsemane	26:36–56	14:32–52	22:39–53	17:1—18:11
Before the Sanhedrin	26:57–68	14:53–65		18:12–14
Peter's denial	26:69–75	14:66–72	22:54–62	18:15–27
The death of Judas	27:1–10			
Jesus before Pilate	27:11–26	15:1–15	23:1–7	18:28–40
Jesus before Herod			23:8–11	
Before Pilate again			23:12–25	19:4–16
The crucifixion	27:32–56	15:21–41	23:26–49	19:17–37
The burial	27:57–66	15:42–47	23:50–56	19:38–42

Introductory tasks

- Imagine you are Peter. Write your diary account for the day you denied Jesus.
- Write the events of Holy Week from the viewpoint of one of the key characters. You might choose Mary the mother of Jesus, Mary Magdalene, or perhaps one of the disciples or a Roman soldier.
- Find out how your local Christian church celebrates the events of Holy Week today.
- Using the Internet, find out how Holy Week is commemorated in other countries.

Key symbols in the story

Palm branches and palm crosses

Palm branches are a reminder that branches were taken from the trees when Jesus entered into Jerusalem on the first Palm Sunday. Each year, in many Christian churches, crosses made from palm leaves are distributed. They represent the fate that was to befall Jesus. In some Christian churches, palm crosses are returned the following year to be burnt to provide the ashes for the Ash Wednesday services.

The donkey or colt

It is significant that Jesus rode into Jerusalem on a donkey. Jesus was treated like a king, but it was the custom at the time of Jesus for kings to ride on horses. Jesus, however, chose to ride on a donkey as a sign of humility.

The jug, bowl and towel

Jesus chose to wash the disciples' feet before the last supper. This reflected Jesus as a servant and was a clear expression of his humility.

Bread

The bread eaten at the last supper would have been the unleavened bread of Passover (*seder*). However, in the Gospel accounts, Jesus changes the words of the *seder* meal at the point where the leader breaks the bread and distributes it, saying, 'Blessed are you, Lord our God, King of the universe, who brings forth bread from the earth'. Jesus broke the bread and then talked about his body, which would be broken. He called his action 'the new covenant' and said, 'Do this in remembrance of me.' These words have been used by Christians ever since, during the service of Holy Communion.

Wine

At Passover, Jewish people drink wine, saying, 'Blessed are you, Lord our God, King of the universe, who chose us from all peoples and exalted us among all the nations, and made us holy with his commandments.' Jesus took the wine and referred to it as a new covenant symbolized by his blood, which was to be shed on the cross. Wine has also become a key symbol of the Eucharist and the way in which Christians remember Jesus.

Thirty silver coins

Thirty silver coins was the price paid for the information leading to Jesus' arrest. This amount of money has become a symbol of betrayal.

Gethsemane

The word Gethsemane means 'olive press'. It was in the garden of Gethsemane, on the Mount of Olives, that Jesus prayed on the night before he was crucified. Olives were traditionally a symbol of peace, but here we have Jesus in the peace of a garden, suddenly disrupted by the noise of the soldiers arriving to arrest him.

The kiss

The Gospels tell us how Judas kissed Jesus to give away his identity to the Roman soldiers who had come to arrest him. Kissing is usually a sign of greeting, affection or love, but in this story it is a symbol of betrayal.

The crown of thorns

The Gospel story tells us how Jesus was stripped, flogged, hit and spat at. Then a crown of thorns was placed on his head. Matthew,

Luke and John tell how the Roman soldiers plaited a crown made out of thorns to place on Jesus' head so that they could mock him as a king.

Purple robe

The purple robe was traditionally a symbol of kingship, but the story tells how the soldiers placed a purple robe around Jesus and mocked him, calling him 'The king of the Jews'.

Crucifixion

Crucifixion was a harsh and cruel punishment used by the Romans. The point about crucifixion in the case of Jesus is that it was the method of execution used for those accused of anti-government rebellion. The Jewish authorities engineered this accusation to ensure that Jesus was crucified. The Bible emphasizes that Jesus' crucifixion was central to his mission but does not record the details of the crucifixion itself. Teachers can find further information on the practice of crucifixion using an Internet search engine.

Sword

The Gospels tell how a sword was used to pierce Jesus' side, to check that he was dead.

Cross

Since the crucifixion, the cross has become the most important Christian symbol.

INRI

These are the initial Latin letters for *Iesus Nazarenus Rex Iudaeorum*, which means 'Jesus of Nazareth, King of the Jews'. This was the inscription over the cross as recorded in John 19:19.

Stations of the cross

Another way of looking closely at the final days of Jesus' life is by using 'The stations of the cross'. These symbols depict the story of his journey to the cross, his death and burial. Many Christian churches have these stages of the journey as paintings or other artworks around the walls of the church building.

Hot cross buns

Hot cross buns have a special symbolic meaning for Christians. They help to tell the story of the crucifixion. The currants represent the nails, the cross reflects the crucifixion and the spices represent not only the smells of the time but also the tears and sadness of the event.

Understanding the story through the senses

Sight

Throughout the centuries, artists across the world have used Holy Week as the inspiration for their work. One of the most famous artworks is the *Pieta* by Michelangelo Buonarroti, which is now kept in the Vatican in Rome. The sculpture shows Mary holding her dead son in her arms. With this statue, Michelangelo gives us a clear view of human suffering. An image can be found on the Internet using a web search engine.

As Mary holds Jesus' lifeless body on her lap, her face shows serenity and an acceptance of her immense sorrow. Mary, who gave birth to this person, now holds his dead body in her arms. Father Giovanni Giuliani's *Guide to St Peter's Basilica* says, 'It seems almost as if Jesus is about to reawaken from a tranquil sleep and that after so much suffering and thorns, the rose of resurrection is about to bloom.'

If you look closely at Mary's face you will see that Michelangelo has shown her as being very young. Over the years he has been criticized for this, since she must have been about 45–50 years old when Jesus died. However, Michelangelo said that he had been thinking of his own mother's face: he was only five when she died and this was how he remembered her.

Look closely at the sculpture. How do you think Mary might have been feeling?

Sound

Reflect on the words of a song for Passiontide, such as 'There is a green hill far away' (HON 499) or 'From heaven you came, helpless babe' (HON 148).

Jerusalem was full of noise in Jesus' final week. The week began with the shouts of 'Hosanna' on Palm Sunday. Then there was the sound of the commotion in the temple, the sounds of the crowds and the sounds at the crucifixion on Good Friday, ending with Jesus' words from the cross and the noise of the earthquake. During the week before his death, Jesus delivered some of his greatest teaching. The chart on page 95 shows where you can find the passages of teaching in each Gospel. You might listen to some of them.

Smell

Throughout Holy Week, the key events would have had their own distinctive smells. First of all, there would have been the donkey and the crowds on Palm Sunday, then the incense in the temple on Monday, the street markets with their spices, the horses of the Roman soldiers and the smell of tortured flesh and excrement at the crucifixion. There was also the smell of the food eaten throughout the week, such as bread, lamb and other food cooked for the Passover meal, as well as the smell of oil lamps burning.

Touch

Think carefully about how the sense of touch comes into this story. We begin with the waving of the palm branches on Palm Sunday, and then Jesus overturns the tables of the money changers in the temple. He was anointed by the woman at Bethany (Matthew 26:6–13 and Mark 14:1–9). On Maundy Thursday, Jesus washed the disciples' feet, broke the bread at the meal, then knelt to pray in the garden of Gethsemane. The story also gives us examples of the pain of touch on Jesus himself. He was kissed by Judas in the garden. He was arrested, flogged, beaten, spat at and had a crown of thorns forced upon his head. He then had to carry the weight of the cross to the place of crucifixion, where he had nails hammered into his hands.

Taste

Explore the food that might have been eaten at the Passover meal, or the food that Christians eat to remember the passion story today, such as hot cross buns. The story also tells how, when Jesus was thirsty on the cross, he was given vinegar to drink.

A focus table of reflection for the classroom

If the classes take up the option in Assembly Two of focusing on just one station of Holy Week, that could become their classroom focus. Another option would be to download various images each day, depicting the events of Holy Week. Each day, add to the table an appropriate artefact from the list provided on pages 106–107.

Consider the following key words:

⊕ Rejection
⊕ Betrayal

- Denial
- Humiliation
- Bullying
- Mocking
- Brutality
- Murder

Ask the pupils to consider the ways in which these words are often re-enacted in today's world, in the classroom, or in the playground. Display the words.

Ask the pupils to write a prayer or read the appropriate passage from the Gospels and reflect on the events that took place. Consider Jesus' words from Matthew 25:45: 'Whenever you failed to help any of my people, no matter how unimportant they seemed, you failed to do it for me.'

Reflecting on the story

Assembly One: A sound montage for Good Friday

The following outline is designed to help pupils appreciate the varying sounds at the time of the crucifixion. Rather than just silence and grief, there would have been other more chaotic sounds from the crowds that gathered there.

You will need:
- An image of the crucifixion, such as *The Crucifixion* by Master of the Parlement de Paris.
- A plain table with a candle but no tablecloth.
- A life-size cross.

- ✥ One child to take the part of the centurion at the foot of the cross (preferably with appropriate dress, such as a Roman soldier's helmet).
- ✥ A piece of wood to tap on the floor to represent the sound of the nails.
- ✥ On a small piece of paper for the centurion, the words 'Truly, this man was the Son of God.'
- ✥ A recording of the words of the hymn 'When I survey the wondrous cross'.
- ✥ Large cards, each one bearing one of the following chants:
  - 'What's the noise? Tell me what's happening.'
  - 'Ha! Ha! Ha! He thought he was the Son of God.'
  - 'What a bit of luck! Throw the dice.'
  - 'If you're so great, come down from the cross.'
  - 'What's gone wrong? We thought he was our Saviour.'
  - 'Look at him, he's dying.'

Suggested opening music and entrance

Children enter to the sound of a Lenten hymn or song, or suitable recorded music. For example:

○ From heaven you came, helpless babe (HON 148)
○ 'Pie Jesu' from *Requiem* by Andrew Lloyd Webber

Christian greeting

Leader: Be with us, Lord Jesus, in the power of your Spirit.
Response: As we now reflect on that first Good Friday.

Introduction

Read the account of the crucifixion from Mark 15:16–39.

Suggested song

There is a green hill far away (HON 499)

Application

Project the chosen crucifixion image on to a screen. Arrange the pupils on the floor around the cross in six separate groups. In each group, have a child holding a large card bearing one of the six chants. Stand the child playing the centurion next to the cross and give him or her the final words to say on a slip of paper. Have one child beat out the rhythm of the nails on wood. This needs to be a steady 'rap, rap, rap' rhythm. As the nail rap continues unabated, get the children to shout out their chants, keeping the first one going while the second starts, and so on until all the six chants together create a cacophony of sound. Maintain for a few seconds, then gradually phase out the first chant, then the second, and so on. When the sixth chant is phased out, keep the sound of the nails going for about ten seconds. Then, in the silence, the child playing the centurion declares, 'Truly, this man was the Son of God.' Hold the silence for a further ten seconds and then play all verses of the hymn 'When I survey the wondrous cross'.

Prayer

Light the candle before saying the following prayer.

Dear God, as we reflect on this most holy week, we remember the first Good Friday when Jesus was brought before Pontius Pilate and condemned to death. We thank you for his courage as he was cruelly tortured and crucified. As we reflect upon the sounds of that day, help us never to forget that Jesus died for us. Amen

Dismissal

Leader: Let us go with hope in our hearts.
Response: As we now look forward to Easter and the resurrection.

Suggested music to exit

There is no music to exit for this assembly, as, on this occasion, the children should be asked to leave in silence as they reflect on the significance of this most holy day.

Optional extras

1 Instead of chants from the crowd of onlookers, choose Jesus' words from the cross that the Gospel writers have recorded, for the children to shout in sequence.
2 Have the children shouting their chants as they move from their separate classrooms and arrive at the foot of the cross, keeping the cacophony of sound going until all are gathered.

Assembly Two: A journey through Holy Week

The following outline takes as its inspiration the traditional stations of the cross. Each of the six stations used represents a stage in the sequence of Holy Week. Through this worship, pupils should gain a better understanding of the gradual unfolding of events throughout this dramatic and holy week. It is suggested that each class should focus on one of the stations, so that each will be focusing on a different aspect of Holy Week as part of its RE curriculum.

You will need:

✣ A series of images to project, each one relating to a 'station' during Holy Week. Possibilities are:

- Station 1: Pietro Lorenzetti's *Entry of Christ into Jerusalem* for Palm Sunday.
- Station 2: Bernardino Mei's *Christ Cleansing the Temple* for Monday of Holy Week.
- Station 3: Leonardo da Vinci's *The Last Supper* for Maundy Thursday.
- Station 4: Sandro Botticelli's *Agony in the Garden* for the night in the garden of Gethsemane.
- Station 5: Domenichino's *The Way to Calvary* for Good Friday.
- Station 6: Peter Paul Rubens' *The Entombment* for the Saturday before Easter.

✣ Three tables, one with a red cloth, one with a white cloth and one without a cloth to symbolize the bareness of the tomb. Place a candle on each table.

Six classes should be prepared, one to present each 'station'. Each class will need to have a reader for their biblical narrative, a reader for the appropriate prayer below, and a range of artefacts relating to that particular station. Appropriate artefacts would be:

❂ Station 1 (Palm Sunday): palm branches, palm crosses, a picture of a donkey (or a donkey mask)
❂ Station 2 (Monday of Holy Week): a bag of money, table, cardboard doves, a seven-branched candelabrum (menorah)
❂ Station 3 (Maundy Thursday): bread and wine, a towel, water jug and bowl, seder plate and unleavened bread (matza)
❂ Station 4 (garden of Gethsemane): olives, olive oil, ornament of praying hands, Roman soldier's costume

- Station 5 (Good Friday): large lightweight cross, crown of thorns, whip, sword, dice, purple material, bag of nails
- Station 6 (Saturday): linen cloth, spices such as frankincense and myrrh, a large stone

Suggested opening music and entrance

Something suitable for the passion story, such as:

- Allegri, *Miserere Mei*
- Franck, *Panis Angelicus*
- Bach, *St Matthew Passion* (excerpts)

Christian greeting

Leader: Come let us walk with Jesus.
Response: As we journey through Holy Week.

Introduction

Remind the children of the six key 'stations' that they will encounter as they journey through Holy Week.

Suggested songs

It is a thing most wonderful (HON 255)
There is a green hill far away (HON 499)

Application

On the table with the red tablecloth, light the candle. Ask each class in sequence to present a 'station' of Holy Week to the other pupils.

- Station 1 (Palm Sunday): Project the image and read Mark 11:1–11. Show the artefacts, explain their significance and place them on the table. A child then reads the following prayer.

Dear God, as we reflect on this most holy week, we remember the first Palm Sunday when Jesus showed great humility by riding into Jerusalem on a donkey. We also remember the crowds that welcomed him with shouts of 'Hosanna'. We pray that we, too, might show humility in our lives and, like the crowds, welcome Jesus into our lives. We pray this as we follow in Jesus' footsteps. Amen

✪ Station 2 (Monday of Holy Week): Project the image and read Mark 11:15–18. Show the artefacts, explain their significance and place them on the table. A child then reads the following prayer.

Dear God, as we reflect on this most holy week, we remember the day when Jesus strode into the temple and, in his anger, threw out the greedy money changers and those selling animals for sacrifice. We pray that, like Jesus, we might show anger at injustice when we see it in our world today. We also pray that we might resist the temptation for us to become greedy at the expense of others. We pray this as we follow in Jesus' footsteps. Amen

✪ Station 3 (Maundy Thursday): On the table with the white tablecloth, light the candle. Project the image and read Mark 14:12–26. Show the artefacts, explain them (refer to John 13:1–9 for the significance of the water, jug, towel and bowl) and place them on the table with the white tablecloth. A child then reads the following prayer.

Dear God, as we reflect on this most holy week, we remember the first Maundy Thursday, when Jesus shared the Passover meal with his friends and showed himself to be a servant by washing their feet. We especially recall how, at the last supper, Jesus asked his friends to remember him as they shared the bread and wine together. We pray, too, that we might be good servants to others and that we, like the disciples, might always remember Jesus when we come together to pray and worship him. We pray this as we follow in Jesus' footsteps. Amen

✪ Station 4 (garden of Gethsemane): Project the image and read Mark 14:32–42. Show the artefacts, explain their significance and place them on the table. A child then reads the following prayer.

Dear God, as we reflect on this most holy week, we remember the night in the garden of Gethsemane when Jesus prayed to you as the disciples slept. We remember the sadness he felt in his heart, but also his trust in you. We remember, too, how Judas betrayed Jesus with a kiss, revealing him to the soldiers and enabling them to arrest him. We pray that, like Jesus, we will always turn to you in prayer. Help us to do our best to follow Jesus and remain his friend. We pray this as we follow in Jesus' footsteps. Amen

✪ Station 5 (Good Friday): Project the image and read Mark 15:6–39. Show the artefacts, explain their significance and place them on the table. A child then reads the following prayer.

Dear God, as we reflect on this most holy week, we remember the first Good Friday, when Jesus was brought before Pontius Pilate and condemned to death. We thank you for his courage as he was cruelly tortured and crucified. We pray now for all those who, like Pilate, have to make difficult decisions about the lives of others. Help them to have the wisdom to see when someone is innocent. We also pray for ourselves, that we are not quick to condemn but that, like Jesus, we have compassion and are able to forgive. We pray this as we follow in Jesus' footsteps. Amen

✪ Station 6 (Saturday before Easter): On the table with no tablecloth, light the candle. Project the image and read Mark 15:42–47. Show the artefacts, explain their significance and place them on the table. A child then reads the following prayer.

Dear God, as we reflect on this most holy week, we remember the first Saturday, when Jesus' body lay in the darkness of the tomb. We remember the disciples, who were devastated to lose their friend. We also remember Jesus' mother, Mary, who could do nothing as her son was crucified and his body laid in the tomb. We pray for all those who mourn the death of a loved one at this time, that they, too, might receive comfort and compassion in their hours of darkness. We pray this as we follow in Jesus' footsteps. Amen

Suggested songs

Were you there when they crucified my Lord? (HON 540)
When I survey the wondrous cross (HON 549)

Dismissal

Leader: Let us go with hope in our hearts.
Response: As we now look forward to Easter and the resurrection.

Suggested music to exit

Either repeat the music used for the entrance, or use one of the other pieces listed.

Optional extras

1 Have six classrooms, each set up as one 'station' of Holy Week, so that your worship becomes nomadic. In each classroom, visiting pupils could experience reading, artefacts and prayers as listed above. Paper footprints on the corridor floor could direct children around the 'stations' to remind them of how Christians follow in Jesus' footsteps.
2 Instead of using tables, the artefacts could be placed on the floor in the shape of a cross.

The story of Easter

Key focus: the resurrection

Background information for the teacher

The word resurrection means to 'rise again'. In Christian terms, it refers to Jesus coming back to life after three days. Each of the four Gospels tells us that Jesus rose from the dead and was seen by his friends. Matthew's Gospel tells us that there was a violent earthquake when the women were visiting the tomb in which Jesus' body had been placed. They saw an angel, who told them that Jesus had risen from the dead and that they should go and tell the other disciples (Matthew 28:1–10). Later, Jesus appeared to the disciples.

Mark tells how, when the women went to embalm Jesus' body, they found the tomb empty and the stone rolled away. Inside they saw 'a young man' wearing a white robe, who told them that Jesus had been raised to life and that they should go and tell the others. Mark goes on to say that Jesus appeared to Mary Magdalene and then the other disciples (Mark 16:1–14).

Luke tells the story once again of how, when the women went to the tomb, they found it empty and the stone rolled away, but this time it is two men 'in shining white clothes' who tell them that Jesus has risen from the dead. Luke goes on to tell how Jesus later appeared to his friends on the road to Emmaus and then to the other disciples (Luke 24:1–49).

In John's Gospel, we have not only the story of Mary Magdalene, who mistook Jesus for the gardener, but also the story of Thomas, who did not believe at first, and how Jesus appeared to his friends in the upper room. Later, John tells how Jesus appeared at Lake Tiberias (another name for Lake Galilee) when Peter and the other disciples were fishing (John 21:1–14).

All four Gospels tell us that Jesus made several appearances before he finally left his earthly existence, but there is also reference to the resurrection in Acts 1:3 and in 1 Corinthians 15:1–7, where Jesus is said to have appeared to over 500 of his followers at one time.

There is no scientific evidence to prove that Jesus rose from the dead, but we know that what took place transformed his friends from frightened, bewildered mourners into powerful preachers. Indeed, many of them were prepared to die for their belief in the resurrection. We also know that the first qualification required to become an apostle was to have seen the risen Lord and to have been a witness of the resurrection.

The liturgical colour for Easter is gold or white, to show that Easter is a key festival.

Exploring the story

Read the story of the resurrection in John 20:1–18. Discuss the pupils' own views and the views of others about the resurrection accounts and life after death. Consider the differences that a belief in the resurrection means for Christians and would mean for others.

Introductory questions about the story

Compare the other Gospel accounts of the resurrection and Jesus' first appearances (Matthew 28:1–20; Mark 16:1–20; Luke 24:1–53).

What are the similarities and what are the differences between these accounts?

Introductory tasks

- ✪ Explore different works of art relating to the resurrection, such as Piero della Francesca's *Resurrection*, or Caravaggio's *Supper at Emmaus*. Consider their similarities, symbolism and differences.
- ✪ Analyse the different Gospel accounts and look for all the opposites and contrasts, such as the details about Jesus asking Mary Magdalene not to touch him (John 20:11–18) and then asking Thomas to touch him (vv. 24–29).
- ✪ Discuss the actions of a spiritual body as opposed to the actions of a physical body—for example, the ability to pass through closed doors (John 20:19) and yet sit and eat food with the disciples (21:9–13).
- ✪ Using the Internet, explore how Christians in other countries celebrate Easter.

Key symbols in the story

The story of the resurrection is filled with symbolism. Above all, Christians believe that the earthly barriers were swept aside and death defeated.

The stone

We see the symbols of the stone rolled away, the empty tomb and the grave clothes left behind. For Christians, this shows that Jesus can overcome all earthly barriers.

Angels

Angels are regarded as God's messengers and in this Easter story they proclaim the message that Jesus is no longer confined to the tomb.

Breaking of bread

After the resurrection, Jesus appears and joins the disciples for a meal. The word 'companionship' means 'breaking bread together'. This is especially clear in Luke's account of the journey on the road to Emmaus, where Jesus is finally recognized by his friends when he breaks the bread (Luke 24:30–31). This action is a key eucharistic symbol for Christians today.

Fish

In both Luke 24:42 and John 21:11–13, Jesus is shown to be eating fish with his friends. The fish became a key Christian symbol and a secret sign for the early Christian Church.

Over the years, Christians have created other symbols to represent the resurrection:

- The empty cross: This reminds Christians that Jesus was crucified and then rose to new life.
- Easter eggs, chicks and bunnies: The Easter story is about new life and resurrection.
- Pomegranates: This fruit is native to the Mediterranean and the lands of the Bible. Used as a sacred symbol in ancient times, because of its many seeds it has become a symbol of fertility and new life. When used as a symbol of resurrection, it is bursting open to expose the seeds. For Christians, it has consequently become a symbol of Christ bursting open the tomb and overcoming death. It is said that the pomegranate has 613 seeds, the same as the number of commandments in Judaism.

✪ Easter bonnets: The wearing of new clothes, including Easter bonnets, is a tradition that originated with the practice of baptizing new believers at Easter. Newly baptized Christians wearing their new clothes are also a symbol of new life.

✪ Candles: These are used by many Christians to represent Jesus as the light of life overcoming the darkness of death.

✪ The Paschal candle: Many Christian churches use a paschal candle to symbolize the resurrection of Jesus from the dead. It is used in many Orthodox, Roman Catholic and Anglican churches on the Saturday night before Easter Day, or early on Easter morning. Sometimes a paschal candle is decorated with the Greek letters alpha and omega, which represent the beginning and the end of time. The cross reminds us that Jesus was crucified and the five incense grains represent the five wounds in Jesus' body (the four nails and the sword). There is also the date of the current year, a reminder of Jesus' continuing presence.

✪ For Christians, the paschal candle symbolizes Christ's victory over death, a light entering the darkness. As the priest lights the candle, he or she declares, 'The light of Christ'. The candle is then taken in procession into the darkened church and members of the congregation light smaller candles from the large one to symbolize Jesus' power over death and darkness.

Understanding the story through the senses

Sight

Many artists have used further symbolism to try to explain the story of the resurrection. Obtain an image of Titian's *Noli me Tangere* ('Do not touch me'). This can be found on the Internet using a web search engine. The picture is based on the story from John 20:11–18. Titian has painted Jesus holding a gardener's hoe because, in the story, Mary mistakes Jesus for the gardener.

The veil wrapped around Jesus represents the veil that hides the dead from the living. The town on the right of the picture shows earthly life—people living and working. The sun is rising on the left to show the risen Christ in light, after the darkness of the tomb. Mary kneels at Jesus' feet in a pose of humility. (The word 'humility' comes from the Latin *humus*, meaning 'earth'.) Under her left hand is the pot of ointment that she was taking to the tomb to anoint the body. If you look closely you can see that Jesus' feet are pierced.

Explore what is happening in the picture.

○ Who are the characters?
○ Where did the artist get his inspiration for the painting?

Sound

Think about the sounds that would have been heard during the resurrection. What would have been the feelings of those who witnessed the resurrection appearances? Would there have been stunned silence or shouts of joy? Matthew tells us that an earthquake occurred at the time of the resurrection (Matthew 28:2). Imagine what sounds it would have prompted. Listen to the words of the hymn 'Thine be the glory'. Write another verse to go with the painting.

Smell

In the story of Epiphany, the wise men took gifts of gold, frankincense and myrrh to the child Jesus (Matthew 2:1–12) (see page 67). The gold represents the kingship of Jesus, but the frankincense and myrrh were used for embalming. The Gospels tell us how Jesus' body was anointed with spices and perfume (John 19:39–41; Mark 16:1; Luke 23:56—24:1). It was the custom at that time for Jewish people to embalm a body in preparation for burial. In accordance with Jewish law, the women waited until the Jewish sabbath (Saturday) had ended before they set out to embalm

Jesus' body. The Epiphany story shows that, even at his birth, the gifts presented to Jesus gave a foretaste of his death.

Touch

Read the story of Thomas (John 21:24–29). Analyse the differences between this story and the story of Mary Magdalene's encounter with the risen Jesus. When Jesus appeared to Mary Magdalene in the garden, he said, 'Don't hold on to me!' whereas when he appeared to Thomas, he asked Thomas to touch him and put his fingers into the wounds, so that Thomas would stop doubting and have faith.

Taste

Think about what happens when we cry. Have you ever tasted your tears? Did they taste salty? Do you think Mary Magdalene would have tasted her tears as she sat weeping beside the empty tomb? Would they have changed to tears of joy? In the resurrection story in both Luke's Gospel and John's Gospel, Jesus shares a meal twice with his disciples. Think about some of the food that is eaten today during the festival of Easter, such as hot cross buns, Easter eggs, Easter biscuits and Simnel cake.

A focus table of reflection for the classroom

The Christian festival of Easter lasts for 50 days, until the feast of Pentecost. This keeps in line with the Jewish festivals of Passover and Shavuot. Schools may like to keep these 50 days special by having a focus table for prayer and reflection in the classrooms. The liturgical colour is gold or white, so either of these could be the colour used for a cloth. As with an Advent calendar, there could be a countdown to Pentecost.

Symbols relating to the resurrection appearances of Jesus could be placed on the table, such as fish, a fishing net, a model boat, bread, wine and so on. Ask the pupils to consider what words might best reflect the shock and surprise of the disciples—for example, 'amazing', 'incredible'. Add one word per day to the table display to give a total of 50 words. These words could be written on a hand shape to remind the children of the significance of hands in the post-resurrection appearances—for example, Jesus breaking bread, the story of Thomas and Jesus' pieced hands, caring hands and so on.

Reflecting on the story

Assembly One: The resurrection

The following reflection aims to help pupils consider how, for Christians, the story of Jesus' resurrection can turn despair to happiness and fear to excitement. As part of the reflection, use one or more key symbols and images of the resurrection as a focal point for a moment of quiet reflection to consider the ideas and emotions linked to the story.

You will need:
+ An image of the resurrection story.
+ Symbols to represent the resurrection, such as an empty cross, an Easter egg, or an Easter chick.
+ A table with a cloth and a candle.
+ A Bible.

Suggested opening music and entrance

- ✪ Be still, for the presence of the Lord (HON 53)
- ✪ From heaven you came, helpless babe (The servant king) (HON 148)
- ✪ He is Lord (HON 204)
- ✪ Thine be the glory (HON 503)

Christian greeting

Leader: Alleluia, Christ is risen.
Response: He is risen indeed. Alleluia!

Introduction

Light the candle (if possible, borrow a paschal candle from a local church) and explain that, for Christians, the paschal candle symbolizes Jesus' victory over death: the light drives out the darkness. Explain the use of the paschal candle at the Easter Eve celebrations (see Easter symbols on page 115) and how it reminds Christians that they, too, have a responsibility to continue to spread the 'light of Christ' into the world today.

Suggested song

Jesus Christ is risen today (HON 267)

Application

Talk about the story of the resurrection and the Christian belief that, through his death and resurrection, Jesus opened the doors of heaven so that those who believe in him can be friends with God in life and eternally after death. Discuss the symbols of resurrection and new life with the pupils and go on to consider the difference belief in Jesus' resurrection might make for Christians. Go on to talk about the different ways that Easter is celebrated in different parts of the world.

Prayer

Dear God, as we join in worship to celebrate the triumph of the resurrection, we pray that our darkness will be turned to light, our despair give way to hope and our fears give way to wonder. May the joy of Jesus' first disciples fill our hearts and may our lives be enriched by your continual presence. Amen

Dismissal

Leader: Go with the risen Christ in your hearts.
Response: Thanks be to God.

Suggested music to exit

Sing John Rutter's 'The Lord bless you and keep you' as a closing song, or play the song as the children exit.

Optional extras

1 Get the children to decorate their own paschal candle with some of the key symbols of Easter. (Paints for model painting work well.)

2 Dramatize the lighting of the paschal candle. First of all, dim the lights in the hall. Then, as the candle is lit (or as it is carried in), someone shouts 'The light of Christ', and all the children make a cacophony of joyous noise using cymbals, bells and other percussion instruments.

Assembly Two: Breakfast on the beach

The following outline helps pupils to appreciate that, following Jesus' death, the disciples went back to their normal lives until they met their risen Lord. Furthermore, pupils will come to an understanding of the significance of the fish as a symbol for early Christians. The Greek word for 'fish' was ΙΧΘΥΣ, pronounced 'ichthus'. These letters became a code for early Christians:

I	=	Iesous	=	Jesus
X	=	Christos	=	Christ
Θ	=	Theou	=	God's
Y	=	Yios	=	Son
Σ	=	Soter	=	Saviour

During the persecution of the early Christian Church, the fish was chosen as a secret sign. One person would draw the outline of a fish on the ground in the dust or sand and, if the other person was also a Christian, they would add the eye.

You will need:
+ Dressing-up materials, enough for seven disciples plus Jesus. A headscarf plus a headband for each person would suffice, but if you are able to add other items, such as robes, beards and so on, that would be even better.
+ Seven chairs or two gymnastics benches to make a boat.
+ A fishing net about 2m square (garden netting will suffice).
+ Sticks and red tissue paper to make a 'fire'.
+ A frying pan with a lid, containing a fresh fish such as a mackerel.
+ A loaf of bread.
+ A large card bearing the fish symbol plus the letters ΙΧΘΥΣ.
+ A table with a white or gold cross and white candle.

Suggested opening music and entrance

☸ A recording of the song 'This joyful Eastertide'

Christian greeting

Leader: Alleluia, Christ is risen.
Response: He is risen indeed. Alleluia!

Introduction

Remind the pupils that, following his resurrection, Jesus appeared to his disciples on several occasions, such as when they were behind closed doors (John 20:19–23), with doubting Thomas (John 20:26–31) and on the road to Emmaus (Luke 24:13–35). In the dramatic presentation that follows, pupils will hear how Jesus met with the disciples for a fish breakfast on the shores of Lake Tiberius (another name for Lake Galilee). The story comes from John 21:1–14.

Suggested songs

Alleluia, Alleluia, give thanks to the risen Lord (HON 24)
This is the day, this is the day (HON 508)

As the song is sung, light the candle.

Application

Dress seven pupils as disciples and another as Jesus. Arrange the disciples inside the 'boat' constructed of the seven chairs (or two benches). They will need the fishing net. At the opposite end of the room to the boat, construct the imitation fire. The person playing Jesus needs to squat by the fire with a frying pan containing the covered fish and a loaf of bread.

Using a narrator reading from John 21:1–14, ask the children to dramatize the reading, casting the net out, catching no fish, spotting Jesus, casting the net over the other side and catching an abundance of fish. One pupil, playing Peter, leaps out of the boat and strides ashore, followed by the others dragging the full net. Jesus invites them to breakfast with him. They sit around the fire. Jesus breaks the bread and distributes it. Then Jesus stands up and holds the fresh fish aloft, declaring, 'Come and eat'.

As the fish is held aloft, the narrator steps forward with the card bearing the fish symbol. The symbol is then explained, pointing out that it became a secret symbol for these disciples and others who came to believe in the risen Lord in the years that lay ahead. Ask the children to trace out the fish symbol on the floor in front of them.

NB: The raw whole fish should be disposed of safely after the enactment and the child who held the fish should be directed to wash his or her hands.

Prayer

Lord Jesus, we rejoice in your resurrection from the dead and we thank you that, after that first Easter Day, you met with the disciples and brought them such joy. Be with us now in your risen power and set our hearts on fire with love for you. Amen

Suggested closing songs

Thine be the glory (HON 503)
Jesus Christ is risen today (HON 267)
Give thanks with a grateful heart (HON 154)

Dismissal

Leader: Alleluia, Christ is risen.
Response: He is risen indeed. Alleluia!

Optional extras

1 Allow the children to have a closer look at the fish as they leave, especially if they seldom see or smell more than fish fingers!
2 Relate this story to the feeding of the 5000 with bread and fish.

The story of Pentecost

Background information for the teacher

The festival of Pentecost, or 'Whitsun' as it used to be known, takes place 50 days after Easter and is regarded as the birthday of the Christian Church. This is because, at Pentecost, the disciples were given the power of the Holy Spirit. The disciples had all gone to Jerusalem to celebrate the feast of Shavuot, an important time when Jewish people remembered that God had given them the gift of the Ten Commandments through Moses.

In the Bible, we find the story of Pentecost in Acts 2:1–13. It tells how the Holy Spirit came to the disciples in wind and fire. This was significant because Jewish people had always regarded wind and fire as being vibrant signs of God's presence and power. So, when the disciples experienced the coming of God's Spirit at Pentecost like a rushing mighty wind and with tongues of fire, they would have felt God's presence and power in a special way. Naturally, they were filled with joy. The reference to 'fiery tongues' (Acts 2:3) is also significant since it brings together the idea of fire as a sign of God's presence with the imagery of tongues as languages. Jerusalem would have been crowded with pilgrims and, as a consequence, many other people became believers; so the Christian Church was born.

Because the disciples were so excited, many in the crowd thought they were drunk, but they were quite sober. It was just that, as the Old Testament prophet Joel had promised, they were filled with the Holy Spirit ('The Lord said... I will give my Spirit to everyone', Joel 2:28). Now the disciples believed that it was happening.

Those who witnessed the event that day were amazed to hear the disciples speak in different languages when the Holy Spirit alighted on them. Everyone understood the disciples clearly. It really did not matter what part of the world they came from. As a consequence, on that one day the good news, or 'gospel', was heard by people of the Jewish faith who had come from many farflung places: from Italy in the west and almost to the borders of India in the east. They all heard the disciples speak in their own languages. No wonder they were amazed.

As a result of what happened in Jerusalem on that first Pentecost, Christians saw new meaning in the festival of Shavuot. Although they honoured Moses, to whom God had given the Ten Commandments, the early Church saw Jesus as bringing a new covenant. They believed that the gift of the Holy Spirit symbolized the 'first fruits' of this new covenant. In time, they also came to see that those who received God's gift of the Holy Spirit were given further 'gifts of the Spirit' to enable them to continue Jesus' work. These gifts are listed by Paul in his first letter to the Corinthians (1 Corinthians 12:4–10 and 28) and to the Romans (Romans 12:6–8). They include faith, healing, miraculous works, prophecy, discernment, speaking in tongues and interpretation, as well as gifts that enable people to minister to others in practical ways, such as serving, encouraging, contributing, performing acts of mercy and helping.

These gifts of the Holy Spirit were understood to vary from one believer to another (Romans 12:6), in contrast to the fruit of the Holy Spirit, which all Christians should manifest without variation (Galatians 5:22–23). The fruits of the Holy Spirit are love, joy, peace, patience, kindness, goodness, faithfulness, gentleness and self-control.

As Pentecost came to be seen as representing a fresh beginning, it became a popular time for being baptized. In time, it became the custom to wear white robes for baptism and, for this reason, Pentecost was also known as 'Whit Sunday', or 'White Sunday'. Because of the link between fire and Pentecost, it comes as no surprise that the liturgical colour for this major festival is red.

Exploring the story

Read the story of Pentecost (Acts 2:1–13). The Jewish people had long believed that the Holy Spirit was God's power working in the world. In Hebrew the word for spirit is *ruach*, meaning the life-giving breath of God. The old English word is *gast*, which gives us the word 'ghost'. In Greek it is *pneuma*, as in 'pneumonia'. When someone dies, we still say that they 'give up the ghost': they lose their breath, their spirit. It is from the word 'spirit' that we get the word 'inspired'. The account in Acts is trying to explain that the disciples had become 'inspired'—that is, filled with the power of God's life-giving Spirit.

The story goes on to say that, whatever took place, it changed those present. They were no longer afraid and in hiding after Jesus' ascension. Instead they were able to go out and preach the good news that Jesus had been raised from the dead, with power and conviction. They spoke in such a way that all of those who heard them preach were able to understand what they were saying. The Jewish festival of Shavuot became a special Christian festival celebrating the gifts of the Holy Spirit and the birth of the Christian Church.

Luke (the author of the book of Acts) also talks about the disciples being able to 'speak in tongues'. This story signifies a reversal of the story of the tower of Babel in Genesis, (11:1–9) where, because of their pride, people lost the ability to speak to each other in a common language and were no longer bound to each other in a common obedience to God's will. In the story of

Pentecost, Luke shows us that it is God's will to join together human beings as one family in peace and harmony, and so the disciples were given the power to communicate with those from different lands once again. The Holy Spirit would enable them to go all over the world spreading the good news about Jesus in ways that people could understand.

Introductory questions about the story

⊗ Why do you think the story of Pentecost is so important for Christians?

Introductory tasks

⊗ Imagine you are Peter. Write down the conversation that you might have had with a friend after the events that took place at Pentecost.
⊗ Imagine you are a newspaper reporter in the crowd. Write your story.
⊗ Find out more about the Jewish festival of Shavuot.
⊗ Using the Internet, explore how Pentecost (Whit Sunday) is celebrated across the world. Likewise, explore the development of the Pentecostal movement.

Key symbols in the story

In the story you will see that Luke uses 'fire and wind' to represent the power of the Holy Spirit.

Wind

The Holy Spirit is described as 'a mighty wind'. The effect of this life-giving energy was very powerful. Think about the wind and the power it contains—from a gentle breeze to a tornado.

Fire

Like wind, fire can have great power. It can be a gentle candle flame or it can cause huge damage, as in forest fires.

The bishop's mitre

A mitre is the hat worn by a bishop. Its shape is meant to represent the tongues of fire described in Acts 2:3, so the mitre becomes symbolic of the power of the Holy Spirit.

Understanding the story through the senses

Sight

Many artists have tried to help us understand this story through art. Obtain an image of *The Pentecost* by El Greco. This can be found on the Internet using a web search engine. In this picture, El Greco tries to show the excitement of the disciples. If you look at the picture closely you can see a dove hovering at the top of the painting and a dome that flows over the disciples to represent God's power. El Greco has also tried to put in the tongues of fire floating above the disciples' heads. You will notice that Mary the mother of Jesus is central to the picture. This reflects Acts 1:14, which tells us that Mary the mother of Jesus often met with the disciples to pray. Mary is usually painted wearing blue, which represents her spirituality.

Read the story of Pentecost in Acts 2:1–13. Does it mention a dove? Why do you think the artist has included a dove in the painting?

Sound

Listen to the words of the song 'Colours of day' (HON 87). What is it trying to say about the day of Pentecost? The story in Acts tells us how the Holy Spirit manifests itself like a 'mighty wind'. Think about the sound and the power of the wind: the sound of a gentle breeze or a powerful whirlwind. Acts also describes how the disciples 'spoke in tongues', telling the good news about Jesus. How would you feel if, suddenly, all around you, people from different countries and continents could understand what you were saying?

You might also imagine the noise of the instruments playing for the festival (see the description below of people walking in procession). At the head of the procession was an ox whose horns had been painted gold and decorated with olive branches. Behind the ox came musicians playing flutes, tambourines and other instruments.

Smell

You might like to sit quietly and watch the flame of a candle as it flickers. Does the candle smell? In the days of the temple in Jerusalem, the farmers and their families took some of the first fruits (usually citrus fruits) and some baked loaves of bread and, meeting up with other families on route, walked to Jerusalem in procession. Think about the smells that might have been present on that day, such as the smell from oil and the smells of the bread and other food cooking for the festival.

Touch

For the Christian Church, the Holy Spirit is passed on by the sense of touch. Christians talk about the warmth of the Holy Spirit touching their lives. Acts 13:1–4 speaks of the Holy Spirit being passed on through the laying on of hands. Throughout the centuries, bishops have confirmed and ordained people using the laying on of hands as a symbolic act of passing on the Holy Spirit.

Taste

It is interesting to know that cheese plays an important part in Christian celebrations of Pentecost or Whitsun. This is linked to the Jewish tradition of making cheese-based dishes such as blintzes (crepes filled with sweetened cottage cheese), cheese dumplings and cheesecakes. The tradition says that, when Moses was given the Ten Commandments, the Israelites found themselves without acceptable (kosher) meats or utensils and so were forced to eat dairy foods. Jewish people still celebrate Shavuot with cheesecakes, ice cream and other dairy products.

A focus table of reflection for the classroom

Cover a table with a red cloth. Place on it a red candle and images of the power of the wind over the land and sea, the power of fire and the power of water.

Talk to the pupils about what Christians call the 'power' of the Holy Spirit. Discuss the power of wind, fire and sea. Explain that there are several images that are used by Christians to reflect the power of God as Holy Spirit, such as wind, water, fire, oil and a dove. Discuss the symbolism of the dove and peace.

Make a template in the shape of a dove. Ask the pupils to draw a dove each and then write on the doves how they would like the Holy Spirit to affect their lives and the world in which they live.

Light the candle and ask the pupils to think about the words that they have written. The following prayer is a North American Indian prayer, which you could use.

O great Spirit, whose voice I hear in the winds and whose breath gives life to the world, hear me. I come to you as one of your many children. I am small and weak. I need your strength and your wisdom.

Reflecting on the story

Assembly One: Gifts of the Spirit

The following outline focuses on the gifts of the Holy Spirit and aims to:

- ❂ help pupils understand that, at the first Pentecost, the disciples were celebrating the Jewish festival of gifts (Shavuot).
- ❂ enable them to appreciate the significance of this story both for the Church and for individuals.
- ❂ help them come to a closer understanding of the Holy Spirit as part of the Trinity.

The early Christians would have been familiar with the idea that God gives gifts of the Holy Spirit because there were similar references in the Old Testament scriptures: for example, Numbers 11:29. The prophet Isaiah also spoke of seven gifts of the Holy Spirit: wisdom, understanding, counsel (the ability to give wise advice), strength, knowledge, fear of the Lord (being in respect and awe of the power of God) and true godliness (reflecting the love of God) (Isaiah 11:2–3). These seven gifts were often symbolized in Jewish worship by seven lamps.

When Jesus left this earth to go back to his Father, he gave spiritual gifts to his followers so that they could continue his work. Some time after the first Pentecost, Paul wrote to the people in Corinth, telling them about these gifts, which included wisdom, knowledge, faith, healing, miracles, speaking and explaining God's message, speaking in strange tongues and explaining what was said

(1 Corinthians 12:1–11). He also wrote to the people of Ephesus, listing some of the gifts that marked people out as having a special work to do as leaders of the church (apostles, prophets, evangelists, pastors and teachers) (Ephesians 4:11). All these gifts of the Holy Spirit are given to individuals to help build up the Christian Church.

You will need:
✣ An image of Pentecost to project, such as El Greco's *The Pentecost*.
✣ A table with a red cloth.
✣ Seven candles to symbolize the flames and the seven gifts.
✣ Seven gift boxes, each containing a folded card with one of the seven gifts of the Spirit written on it. Choose either the seven gifts listed in Isaiah 11:2–3 or seven from the list of gifts in 1 Corinthians 12:7–11.
✣ Twelve red ribbons or flags for children to wave.
✣ A Bible.

Suggested opening music and entrance

❂ *Finlandia* by Sibelius

You might also have twelve children waving red ribbons or flags at the entrance to the hall, so that the other children pass through an archway of 'flames'. Project the Pentecost image on to a screen at the same time so that there is a focal point on arrival.

Christian greeting

Leader: The Lord is here.
Response: His Spirit is with us.

Introduction

Talk about the Jewish festival of Shavuot, often called the 'festival of gifts' because it celebrates the giving of the Ten Commandments to Moses. Explain that the disciples were members of the Jewish faith and would have been celebrating this special festival when the events of Pentecost took place.

Read the story from Acts 2:1–13, using either a modern version of the Bible such as the Contemporary English Version or a child's Bible such as *The Barnabas Schools' Bible* (Barnabas, 2007), and talk about how the artist illustrated this event in the chosen projected image. Help the children to make the link between someone filled with the 'breath of God' and being filled with the Holy Spirit: to be filled with life, or to be inspired. You could make links with the words of the Christian creed: 'I believe in the Holy Spirit, the Lord, the giver of life'.

Explain that the events at Pentecost, with flames of fire and a rush of wind, had a dramatic effect on the disciples. No longer were they afraid and in hiding after Jesus' death. Instead, they were confident and boldly preached the good news that Jesus had been raised from the dead. They received a special gift of being able to speak in such a way that people from all parts of the known world could understand what they were saying in their own language.

Explain how the gift of the Holy Spirit to the disciples at Pentecost marks the birthday of the Christian Church. The original Jewish festival, celebrating the gifts of the Ten Commandments, thus became a special Christian festival celebrating the gift of the Holy Spirit. Remind the children that there are other gifts of the Holy Spirit. Some of them are listed in the Old Testament (by the prophet Isaiah), but later Paul reminds the early Christians that there are other gifts of the Holy Spirit that can enrich their lives.

Suggested songs

Come, Holy Ghost, our souls inspire (HON 92)

For I'm building a people of power (HON 135)
Light up the fire (HON 87)

Application

Talk to the children about the giving and receiving of gifts. Try to move them away from materialistic ideas to see that there are other gifts which can be more special, such as the gift of wisdom. Explain that these gifts from God were very special as they had a life-changing effect on the disciples and early Christians.

Using seven children, give each child a gift box with a card inside showing one of the gifts (see 'You will need' list above). Open each box individually and talk about the gift and how it might have changed the lives of those who received it—for example, the ability to give wise advice or perform miracles. Place the name of the gift on the table in front of each of the seven candles, lighting each candle as you proceed. Ask the children to reflect upon their own lives and what gifts they might already have that could help change someone's life for the better—for example, kindness or gentleness.

Prayer

Dear God, the story of Pentecost reminds us that you want us to do our best with the gifts that you give us. Help us to use our gifts wisely and to make the right choices as we journey through life. Amen

Suggested closing song

Light up the fire (HON 87)

Dismissal

Leader: Go in the power of God's Holy Spirit.
Response: To live and work to God's praise and glory.

Suggested music to exit

Exit to the same music played for the entrance. The children can process out through the archway of waving ribbons or flags.

Optional extras

1 Talk about how it is just as important to accept and unwrap a present that has been given to us as it is to give a gift to someone else.
2 Talk with the children about which gifts they would like to receive for themselves, and for what reason.

Assembly Two: Fruit of the Spirit

This outline aims to help children appreciate:

○ symbols of the Holy Spirit.
○ the unpredictability of the movement of the Holy Spirit.
○ the fruit of the Holy Spirit.

You will need:
✣ A table with a red tablecloth and red candle.
✣ A branch from a tree, about 1.5m high, on which are suspended nine different paper fruits (such as an orange, an apple and so on). Each paper fruit should be about 5 cm in size and labelled with a 'fruit of the Spirit' as listed in Galatians 5:22–23 (love, joy, peace, patience, kindness, goodness, faithfulness, gentleness and self-control).
✣ A kite. This could be either purchased in advance or made in the classroom. It should be painted red with additional painted symbols of the Holy Spirit, such as a dove and flames of fire.
✣ An image of a dove or a flame to project.

Suggested opening music and entrance

❂ *The Lark Ascending* by Vaughan Williams

Christian greeting

Leader: The Lord is here.
Response: His Spirit is with us.

Introduction

Explain that the early Christians who were filled by God's Holy Spirit not only received gifts of the Spirit such as wisdom, understanding, counsel (the ability to give wise advice), strength, knowledge, fear of the Lord (respect and awe for the power of God) and true godliness (reflecting the love of God). They also found that they developed a variety of fruits of the Holy Spirit. These fruits are listed in Galatians 5:22–23. They are love, joy, peace, patience, kindness, goodness, faithfulness, gentleness and self-control. Read this passage to the children. Show them that these nine fruits of the Holy Spirit can be seen hanging on the tree branch provided.

Talk to the children about which of these spiritual fruits they would particularly like to develop in their own lives, and why. Which of the fruits do they value most in their friends?

Suggested songs

Let there be love shared among us (CFW 58)
Light up the fire (HON 87)

As the song is sung, light the red candle on the table.

Application

Show the children the kite and explain the symbols for Pentecost painted on it. Remind them that the dove is a symbol because of the reference in the Bible to a dove alighting on Jesus' head at his baptism (Mark 1:9–11). The dove has also become a symbol for peace and reconciliation. Likewise, the flame is a symbol for the Holy Spirit because of the story of flames appearing on the heads of the disciples at Pentecost when they received the gift of the Holy Spirit (Acts 2:3).

Invite the children to look at the flame burning on the candle. It looks so small, yet it contains such power. When a flame is out of control, it can destroy houses and even forests. Fire is therefore a symbol of both the unpredictability and the power of God's Holy Spirit at work in the world, and it is not surprising that the liturgical colour for Pentecost in the Church is red.

Explain that the kite is also a good symbol for Pentecost since it is earthbound until it is lifted by the wind and set free. Furthermore, a kite, like the Holy Spirit, is unpredictable in its movements. It goes where the wind blows, for its power comes from the wind. (This could be related to the story of Nicodemus in John 3:6–8.) Choose some children to remove the nine paper fruits from the tree and attach them to the kite's surface. Ask a child to hold up the kite for all to see.

Prayer

Dear God, we thank you that by following Jesus we, too, can reveal the fruits of your Holy Spirit in our lives. Give us a healthy appetite for these fruits so that we might have our lives enriched by love, joy, peace, patience, kindness, goodness, faithfulness, gentleness and self-control. Amen

Suggested closing song

Spirit of God, unseen as the wind (CFW 609)

Dismissal

Leader: Go in the power of God's Spirit.
Response: To live and work to God's praise and glory.

Suggested music to exit

The children may exit to the same music as the entrance music. Ask
a child to carry the kite and lead the rest of the children outside the
school. Once outside, fly the kite so that the symbols of Pentecost
and the fruits of the Spirit can soar skywards. Encourage the
children to think about the great excitement of the first day of
Pentecost.

Optional extras

1 Invite the children to try playing various wind instruments. (You
   might make the link between flutes and the ancient traditions
   of Shavuot.) Remind them that it is breath that enables wind
   instruments to function and make beautiful sounds.
2 Still the children so that they can hear their own breathing.
   Remind them that as breath gives life, so it is with the Spirit of
   God.

The Church today:
The concept of reflective living

Most people think of the 'church' as being a building, but that is just the place where the people happen to meet. The Church today is made up of innumerable individuals, both young and old, who have not only developed a belief in and love of God, but have also decided to be baptized and follow in the footsteps of Jesus as his disciple today. They are known as the 'body of Christ'. Within this 'body' there are also people who are seeking a faith and exploring their understanding of Christianity.

However, being a Christian and a member of the body of Christ is not only about believing in Jesus. It is about a journey, beginning with the rite of passage that Christians call baptism. In this section of the book, we shall examine the practice of baptism and what it means to be a Christian disciple today, travelling on that journey. There are several other Christian rites of passage that those who belong to the Church are likely to experience as they grow and journey. They are called 'sacraments'.

A very useful definition of a sacrament is 'an outward and visible sign of something that is inward and spiritual'. Each sacrament has its own symbol, or sign—something that is outward and visible which helps to provide a simple way of expressing an inner meaning. These symbols are:

- Water for baptism
- Bread and wine for Holy Communion

- Rings for matrimony
- Laying on of hands for confirmation and ordination
- Holy oil for anointing those who are ill, and for reconciliation

Although not all Christians will receive all of these sacraments during their lifetime of belonging to the Christian Church, most will experience the sacrament of baptism.

Central to the life of the Christian Church is the sacrament of Holy Communion, so its significance will be investigated, particularly in relation to how it energizes Christians for their everyday life in the world. Being a Christian also involves following the teachings of Jesus and living out our lives following Christian values such as forgiveness, compassion and so on. Therefore, at the heart of Christian discipleship there is not only a desire to love God, but also a desire to love others as much as we love ourselves. In this section of the book, we will consider what informs the behaviour of the Church as a whole and of Christians as individuals.

The following image is a useful way to illustrate the concept of the Church and the body of Christ.

Illustration: © Patrycja Peslak
Used under licence from Shutterstock, Inc.

The journey of life: belonging and believing

Key focus: Baptism

Background information for the teacher

Christianity is a living, growing faith. There are more Christians in the world today than there have ever been. There are about two thousand million Christians, and many more people become members of the Christian Church every day. In Africa almost 17,000 people become Christians every day. It is clear, then, that the Church is not just a building—it is a group of people who come from many different backgrounds but who all share a common faith in Jesus Christ.

There are Christians in nearly every country in the world. A group of Christians who meet together are called a 'church'. There are many different styles of worshipping Jesus. These different styles are known as denominations. There are over 20,000 denominations: for example, the Orthodox Church, Pentecostals, Anglicans, Roman Catholics, Baptists, Methodists and many more. Whatever their denomination, Christians all worship Jesus and try to live by his teachings in their own way. They are all part of God's family. The point of entry into that family is marked by baptism.

Baptism is just one of seven 'rites of passage' for Christian believers. These rites are commonly called 'sacraments'. The two major sacraments are baptism and Holy Communion (which is also known as the Eucharist, the Mass or the Lord's Supper). These two major sacraments are recognized by all Christians because they were initiated by Jesus himself. The other five sacraments are holy matrimony, confirmation, anointing those who are unwell with oil, ordination and reconciliation. These are regarded as sacraments mainly by Christians from the Roman Catholic, Anglican and Orthodox traditions.

Exploring the story

Read 1 Corinthians 12:12–28. This passage talks about the Church as a body, with each part playing a vital role that makes the body function well. Although feet, hands, eyes and ears are all separate and have separate jobs, together they create an exceptional machine. Even those parts that appear to be weak and soft, like the eye, are indispensable; if they are missing, they force other parts of the body to work harder. 'God put our bodies together in such a way that even the parts that seem the least important are valuable' (1 Corinthians 12:24).

Think of some things we must do to keep our bodies healthy. One is to keep ourselves clean by using water to wash; so, too, with the body of the Christian Church. Christians begin their journey by baptism. Baptism symbolizes a fresh start, washing away the things that displease God. People can be baptized at any age. In some churches today a font (usually a stone basin) is used, and, in others, a baptistery, which is like a small pool. In a baptistery the person being baptized is fully immersed by the water.

In non-conformist churches the baptism service can be quite simple, but in most Anglican churches it can be more elaborate. For example, the priest might use a scallop shell to pour water over the person's head three times, in the name of God the Father, Son and Holy Spirit. The scallop shell is a symbol of pilgrimage, reflecting the fact that at baptism people begin their spiritual journey as Christians. During the service, the candidate is signed with the sign of the cross, often using olive oil that has been blessed for the purpose. Older candidates then have to express their belief in God as Father, Son and Holy Spirit using the words of the creed. If the candidate is a baby, responsible adults express the creed on behalf of the child.

Paul calls the Church 'the body of Christ', brought together by baptism. In 1 Corinthians 12:27 he says that each person contributes to the whole body. Part of what it means to be the body of Christ is to journey out into the world, spreading the good news about Jesus.

Introductory questions about the story

⊕ Why do you think Christians think it is important to mark a person's entry into the Christian Church with the sacrament of baptism?

Introductory tasks

⊕ Design an altar frontal or a stained-glass window to reflect the idea that the Church is not the building but individual Christians across the world.

⊕ Write a poem to reflect the idea that the Church is the body of Christ.

⊕ Consider the ways in which Christians today use parts of their body to follow the teachings of Jesus—for example, by praying or helping others.

⊕ Find an order of service for baptism. Rewrite it using your own words, phrases, hymns and music.

⊕ Find out how baptism and confirmation are celebrated across the world in the different Christian traditions.

Key symbols in the story

Water

Water is a symbol of cleansing, and of a fresh start. It is also life-giving.

Scallop shell

A scallop shell is often used to pour water over the candidate's head in a baptism service. The scallop shell is the symbol of St James, the patron saint of pilgrims. For Christians, baptism is the start of their Christian journey, following in the footsteps of Jesus. This journey is both an outward physical journey and an inward spiritual one.

Candle

A lit candle symbolizes Jesus as the light for the world. Throughout history the light of a candle has symbolized God's presence.

Cross

The cross is the traditional symbol of the Christian Church, chosen because Jesus died on a cross.

Oil

Sometimes candidates are also anointed with olive oil immediately following their baptism. Symbolically, oil gives wisdom and strength. This is equivalent to the anointing of kings and queens at their coronation, where the symbolism is both royal and priestly. The olive is a sacred fruit and the oil has been used for centuries for healing and anointing.

Understanding the story through the senses

Sight

Find an image of a traditional church ceiling, such as the one in Winchester Cathedral. If you turn the picture upside down, you will see that the ceiling looks like a wooden boat. The main part of the cathedral, under this ceiling, is called the 'nave', from the Latin word *navis* meaning 'ship'. When we climb on board a ship, we usually embark on a journey.

So, too, with Christians: when they are baptized they begin a journey. This journey is both an outward physical journey, like the one on a ship, but also an inward spiritual journey. In many traditional Christian churches, the font, used for baptism, is found by the door as you enter. The word 'font' comes from the Latin *fons* meaning 'spring of water'. It is related to the English word 'fountain'.

When we go on a journey on a ship, the waters can be calm or rough. So, too, with the Christian journey, but Christians believe that Jesus and his teachings are with them, steering the ship and guiding them on their journey so that they will never feel alone.

Christians also use their eyes to admire the wonder and mystery of God's creation.

Sound

The Latin word *credo* means 'I believe'. The early Christians tried to set down their key beliefs in a 'creed' or statement of belief. By AD400 there were two main creeds in Christianity: the Apostles' Creed and the Nicene Creed. Both express the key Christian beliefs and are still used in churches today. They are always used in a service of baptism. Listen carefully to the words of the Apostles' Creed (this can be found using an Internet search engine). What does it tell you about Christian belief and what it means to be a Christian?

Smell

In 1 Corinthians 12:17 we read, 'If our bodies were only an eye, we couldn't hear a thing. And if they were only an ear, we couldn't smell a thing.' Imagine not being able to smell beautiful flowers, plants and wonderful foods. What would the world be like? It is our sense of smell that tells us when food is not good to eat or when there is gas or fire nearby that could harm us. Our noses might look strange, but they play a vital role in making our world special and keeping us safe as we journey through life.

Touch

In some Christian churches, baptism takes place when children are small or when they are babies; in other churches it takes place when they are adults and can make the commitment for themselves. In those churches where babies are baptized, there is an additional sacrament that takes place when the candidates are old enough to answer the questions for themselves. This is called 'confirmation', which means 'strengthening', and candidates take on the full responsibility of being a Christian. During confirmation, a bishop will place his hands on the candidate's head and say, 'Confirm, O Lord, your servant… with your Holy Spirit.'

You might also consider other ways in which we use touch as we travel through life, and the ways in which some Christians use touch to follow Jesus (for example, to comfort others or to promote healing).

Taste

Think of the different tastes that we enjoy and value in our daily physical life. Now think of the tastes associated with the journey of faith, such as bread and wine during Holy Communion. For Christians, these are life-giving symbols of their faith and of the presence of Jesus.

A focus table of reflection for the classroom

Read the opening of the story of Dick Whittington, where he sets off for London feeling alone and afraid. Often, in the storybook, there is a picture of Dick sitting by a milestone. Before modern road signs were used, milestones were set along the road at regular intervals. They helped travellers in coaches, on horseback or on foot to see how many miles they had travelled and how far they had to go to reach their destination. Milestones can still be found today on ancient roads. We also use the word to mean the end of a significant stage of life.

Set up a table and use some bricks or painted cereal boxes to represent some milestones in life. Ask the children to name them (for example, birth, starting school and so on). Talk about the milestones that Christians may have in their lives, such as baptism, confirmation, Holy Communion, marriage and so on. Add these words to the milestones.

Listen to the words of the hymn 'Journey of life' by Valerie Collison (CFW 210). It begins by reminding us that the journey through life, though it may appear to be easy, is often very difficult. Christians believe that many dangers and temptations may come their way in life, but if they turn to Jesus for help and support they will get to their destination safely.

Add a symbol for each milestone, such as a scallop shell for baptism. Each day you might read the following prayer or ask the children to write one.

As we journey onward through our lives, through the good times and the bad, help us never to lose sight of the shelter of your loving arms. As we make decisions at different stages of our lives, help us to know that you will always be there. Amen

Reflecting on the story

Assembly One: Reflecting the characteristics of God

This act of worship will enable children to see that the Church is made up of individual people from varying backgrounds and with a variety of interests and occupations. Furthermore, as the body of Christ, Christians not only work together but also reflect a number of the characteristics of God.

You will need:

- A table, tablecloth and candle.
- An image of a church building to project.
- Various props so that children can identify people with specific occupations or hobbies. These could include hats, uniforms or objects associated with the occupation. Individuals will need to come forward to be recognized. Occupations and hobbies should include a mother or father (with, for example, a baby in arms), nurse, chef, fire fighter, teacher, police officer, sculptor or artist, window cleaner, scientist, postal worker, child football supporter, Brownie or Cub.

Suggested opening music and entrance

- A recording of 'Dem bones, dem bones, dem dry bones'

Project an image of a church building on the screen.

Christian greeting

Leader: Come, let us worship our God.
Response: For we are his children, the people of God.

Introduction

Refer to the image. Explain that the Church of God is not a building, but the people of God. The people just happen to meet in a building that is called a church. Even if the church building did not exist, the people who worship in it would still continue to be the Church. Read 1 Corinthians 12:12–27. Explain that the Church is the body of Christ and that all members of the Church have a part to play.

Application

Now introduce, one by one, individuals who might be members of a church congregation and show how each one represents to us a characteristic of God.

- A mother or father reveals to us the love of God.
- A nurse reminds us that God cares for us and longs to heal us.
- A chef reminds us that God provides for our daily needs.
- A fire fighter reminds us that God rescues us in times of difficulty.
- A teacher reminds us that God longs to teach us his ways.
- A police officer reminds us that God expects us to obey his rules and follow his advice.
- A sculptor or artist reminds us that God created the world.
- A window cleaner reminds us that God wants to wash away our sins and give us a fresh start.
- A scientist reminds us that God longs for us to discover more of his creation and for us to be co-creators with him.
- A postal worker reminds us that God communicates with us.
- A football supporter reminds us that God supports us through good and bad times.

❂ A Brownie or Cub reminds us that God longs for us to have friendship and fun with one another.

Next, ask all these individuals to gather around the table (some kneeling in front). Light the candle.

Prayer

Dear God, we thank you for all these people who help to make life so good for us. Help us never to take them for granted. We thank you that they are all members of your body, the Church, and that in their different ways they each remind us of you and of your ways. Show us, too, what we might do to contribute to the life of your Church and become more active members of the body of Christ. Amen

Suggested closing songs

Bind us together, Lord (HON 60)
For I'm building a people of power (HON 135)

Dismissal

Leader: We are the body of Christ.
Response: Let us work together with joy in our hearts.

Suggested music to exit

Exit to the recording of 'Dem bones, dem bones, dem dry bones'.

Optional extras

1 Invite professional people from the local community to attend, wearing their actual uniforms.
2 Talk about church buildings and what they say to us about the nature of God (for example, majestic, peaceful and so on).

Assembly Two: The 'journey of life' life cycle

This assembly will enable children to experience the range of rites of passage that Christians may encounter on their journey through life. It will include a consideration of the key sacraments of the Church. We need to recognize, however, that not all of these sacraments may be experienced in a single person's life. For example, not all will get married and not all will be ordained.

You will need:

✣ A round, white tablecloth and a large candle.

✣ Eight individuals, each carrying a symbol expressing eight different rites of passage, as follows. Each person should have a large label on their back naming the rite they represent.

- Baptism: a baptismal shell and baptismal candles.
- Confirmation: a symbol of the Holy Spirit, such as a dove.
- Eucharist: bread and wine.
- Marriage: wedding rings.
- Ordination: a priest's stole, or a Bible.
- Reconciliation: a cross.
- Anointing those who are unwell: bottle of olive oil.
- Funeral: a jar of earth.

Suggested opening music and entrance

○ 'Rhythm of life' from the musical *Sweet Charity*
○ 'Sunrise sunset' from the musical *Fiddler on the Roof*

Christian greeting

Leader: Praise God who loves us.
Response: Praise God who cares for us.

Introduction

Spread the tablecloth on the floor and place the candle in the centre of the cloth. Explain that you are now going to take a journey through life, looking at key events of religious importance.

Application

Invite the eight chosen individuals to come forward, one at a time, in the sequence listed above (beginning with baptism). Arrange the eight children in a circle around the tablecloth, facing outwards. As each person arrives, ask him or her to reveal their symbol. Explain each symbol to the children, then talk about the significance of that moment in a Christian's life, and the part the Church plays.

When all eight children are in place, ask them to place their symbols in sequence on the tablecloth around the candle. Next, ask them to return to their circle, facing inwards and linking hands. Now ask them to rotate around the tablecloth so that the other children can see the cycle of life in motion. The labels on the backs of the eight children will remind them of the sequence. Then ask the eight children to kneel facing the symbols as you light the central candle.

Prayer

Dear God, we thank you for the many blessings that we receive throughout our lives from the beginning to the end. Guide us as we journey through life and help us to see that you are with us at every moment and that you want the very best for us. Amen

Suggested closing song

The journey of life (CFW 210)

Dismissal

Leader: Let us continue on our journey through life.
Response: Knowing that God loves us and cares for us.

Suggested music to exit

Exit to a recording of 'Rhythm of life' or 'Sunrise sunset'.

Optional extras

1 The person representing reconciliation could shake hands with others in the circle as well as revealing the cross as a symbol.
2 Take the opportunity to explain what a sacrament is (see the definition on page 141).

The journey of life: sharing and caring

Key focus: The Eucharist

Background information for the teacher

For many families, Sunday lunch is still a special time when they all eat together. It is a time for sharing and for fellowship. Others have special meals at Christmas or at other times of celebration when friends or family meet. Christians see themselves as one large family, so they, too, like to meet together and share special meals, just as Jesus did with his friends. Thus Christians often meet together to share a meal, such as at harvest or other celebratory times of year. There is, however, one particular special meal that Christians are obliged to participate in, since it was a command of Jesus to his followers to do so. This special meal is called Holy Communion (also known as Eucharist, Mass or the Lord's Supper). The word 'communion' is particularly apt, since the word means 'joining together' and gives Christians a sense of unity with one another.

In most churches, Holy Communion is celebrated at least once a week, but in others it could be every day. As Christians share this special meal together, they listen to some Bible stories, sing hymns and say prayers. Then, just as Jesus did at the last supper, the priest takes the bread, blesses it and breaks it to share with the congregation. The priest then takes the wine, blesses it and shares it in the same way. By sharing the bread and wine, the family of the Christian Church remembers Jesus and so draws closer to him, just as we share meals with our families at home and grow closer to them.

The bread and wine used in Holy Communion help Jesus to come alive for Christians today because, mysteriously, Jesus is powerfully present with them in those two everyday symbols. Furthermore, just as the food we eat day by day provides energy for our physical activities, so Christians find that the bread and wine received during Holy Communion energizes them for their spiritual journey with God.

At the end of the Communion service, the priest blesses the congregation and then sends them out in the power of God's Holy Spirit, using such words as 'to live and work to God's praise and glory' or 'go in peace to love and serve the Lord'. This is a reminder that Christians are called to go out into the everyday world energized by the communion they have received and taking with them what they have seen and heard in the service. Christians thus go out strengthened with the Holy Spirit and trying to do God's will until they next meet for Holy Communion.

Exploring the story

For Jewish people, the feast of Passover is a key religious festival that remembers the story of Moses leading the Israelites from slavery into freedom. At the time of Jesus, thousands of people would have gone to Jerusalem to celebrate this annual event. The story of Jesus celebrating this meal with twelve of his closest friends can be found in all four Gospels: Matthew 26:17–30; Mark 14:12–26; Luke 22:7–23 and John 13:1–20.

Read the story in Luke 22:7–23. Here we have Jesus continuing the Jewish tradition, but in verses 19–20 Jesus changes the words. At the point in the *seder* (Passover) meal where the leader breaks the matzah bread, Jesus says, 'This is my body, which is given for you. Eat this as a way of remembering me!' In the same way, with the wine, the traditional words of blessing are changed to 'This is my blood. It is poured out for you, and with it God makes his new agreement.' Just as families celebrate special events together, so, too, Christians today remember this event in a special meal called the Eucharist, which comes from the Greek word *eucharisto*, meaning 'thanksgiving'. Just as Jesus did, the priest takes the bread, blesses it and breaks it to share with those present. The priest then takes the cup of wine, blesses it and shares it in the same way. This special act helps Jesus to come alive for Christians today.

Introductory questions about the story

❂ Why is this story so important for Christians today?

Introductory tasks

❂ Read the different Gospel accounts of this story. Outline the similarities and the differences.
❂ Find out about a Passover *seder* and then imagine you were one of the disciples present at the last supper. Write your diary account of the events that took place. Explain how you might have felt.
❂ Interview a local priest about the structure of the Eucharist (also known as Holy Communion, the Mass or the Lord's Supper). Write a booklet explaining this special service to Key Stage 1 pupils, saying why it is important for Christians today.
❂ Find out how different denominations across the world celebrate this special event.

Key symbols in the story

Matzah bread

Matzah bread is unleavened bread used in a Passover *seder*. It represents the unleavened bread that the Israelites were commanded to eat when they fled from Egypt.

Wine

The fruit of the vine has always been regarded as a sacred fruit. In the Passover *seder*, it is a symbol of freedom.

Bread

In many Christian churches, unleavened bread is still used to celebrate Holy Communion. It is sometimes called the 'host', from the Latin word *hostia* meaning *victim*. However, in some churches, ordinary leavened bread is now used as a symbol of what is ordinary in our lives. In the service of Holy Communion, Christians believe that God takes what is ordinary and makes it sacred.

Understanding the story through the senses

Sight

Throughout the centuries, artists across the globe have tried to capture the story of the last supper in paint. One of the most famous paintings is *The Last Supper* by Leonardo da Vinci, painted in the 15th century. This can be found on the Internet using a web search engine.

If you look closely at the painting you will notice that Leonardo has tried to capture the moment when Jesus has told the disciples that one of them would betray him. All twelve disciples are still present. Jesus is at the centre of this human turmoil and Leonardo has painted him with arms outstretched, gesturing to both bread and wine: 'This is my body, this is my blood'. His right hand is extended as if in blessing, whereas his left hand is open in acceptance of the fate that is to befall him.

Although, for Christians, Jesus is the incarnate Son of God, here he is seen to be eating a familiar meal with friends. God is personally present. In the picture, Judas is holding the money bag in his right hand and takes bread with his left, the gesture that identifies him as the betrayer. Thomas is on Jesus' left side, raising his index finger as if asking a question. This same finger he will later place into Jesus' wounds, after the resurrection.

Sound

Two of the key features of a Eucharist are listening and speaking to God. Christians listen to readings from the scriptures. Bells are used in some churches to draw the congregation's attention to the key parts of the service. Music is also used to create an atmosphere and to praise God.

Smell

In some churches, incense is used to heighten the sense that something really special is happening. It is traditionally used to honour sacred objects, in this case the bread and wine and the altar.

Touch

The service contains a special section called 'sharing the peace', during which the members of the congregation turn to each other and shake hands as a sign that they are reconciled to each other. The word 'reconcile' means 'to bring back into friendship'. It would not be right to receive Holy Communion bearing a grudge against another person.

Taste

During Holy Communion the priest breaks the bread and it is shared around. The wine is also shared in the same way. This is to remember the actions of Jesus at the last supper. The word 'companionship' means 'breaking bread together'.

A focus table of reflection for the classroom

You will need:
- ✣ An empty desk.
- ✣ A white tablecloth.
- ✣ Two candlesticks.
- ✣ A wine goblet or a chalice.
- ✣ Red grape juice or a wine bottle.
- ✣ A plate or a paten.
- ✣ A loaf of bread or unleavened matzah bread.

Talk to the pupils about how you might set the table if you had an important guest coming for a special meal. Explain to the pupils that Christians believe that Jesus is regarded as the 'special guest' at Holy Communion. Begin to set the table with a white cloth, candlesticks, bread, wine and a cross.

Read John 6:48–51, where Jesus describes himself as 'living bread' and John 15:1–10, where Jesus says that he is like a vine. Explain why Christians break bread together and drink wine at a service of Holy Communion. Reflect on the words of either the song 'I am the vine, you are the branches' (WGS Vol. 3, p. 52) or the song 'I am the bread of life' (HON 222).

Make a vine branch, draping it over the table and making it climb up the wall so that it looks as if it is growing. Ask the pupils to take a piece of paper, draw around their feet, and then write on the paper what they might do if they were to follow Jesus' teachings and help the kingdom of God grow (for example, be kind to their friends, be helpful to their parents, and so on). Make a path by attaching the paper feet to the vine branches.

Reflecting on the story

Assembly One: A silent Eucharist

The following outline will enable pupils to understand the structure of the Eucharist service. It is most appropriate at the end of a unit of work focused on the Eucharist. It uses symbol and silence rather than lots of words. It is best done as a class worship rather than for the whole school, but an open space is needed.

You will need:
- ✤ A large table for an altar.
- ✤ An image of the last supper to project.
- ✤ A box containing the following items, which will be put on the altar:
  - A tablecloth.
  - Two candles.
  - A Bible.
  - A loaf of bread.
  - A wine bottle filled with grape juice (with cork replaced).
  - Two wine goblets.
- ✤ A second box containing the following items, needed by the leader during the presentation:
  - A white balloon.

- A red felt-tipped pen.
- A small pad of plain paper.
- Two small baskets.
- Two bottles of bubble-making liquid (or a bubble gun).
- Some small bells (sanctuary bells are perfect).
- An inflatable globe of the world (deflated).
- A photo frame without a photo.
- A picture of a church.
- A basket of small pebbles.
- Two garlands of artificial flowers (Hawaiian style).
- A corkscrew (the type with two arms that come up).
- A white sheet (about one square metre).
- A crown of thorns.
- A few white serviettes.

Suggested opening music and entrance

Children enter to a gathering song or a Communion hymn.

❂ Be still, for the presence of the Lord (HON 53)
❂ Gather around for the table is spread (HON 152)

Project an image of the last supper on to a screen.

Christian greeting

Leader: Come, let us meet the risen Lord.
Response: In the breaking of bread.

Introduction

Explain that we will explore the structure of the Eucharist through symbol and silence. Some basic instructions are needed as follows.

- ✪ As a symbol of the Holy Spirit, form the shape of a dove by linking the thumbs of two outstretched hands. Raise and lower like a dove ascending and descending.
- ✪ To signify God, point to the sky; to signify Jesus, stretch arms as if on a cross.
- ✪ To signify belief, touch the head and then the heart.
- ✪ To signify us listening to God, point to everyone, then place a hand behind an ear in a hearing gesture and point to the sky.
- ✪ To signify God speaking to us, point to the sky with one hand, then place the closed fingertips of that hand to your lips. Make a sweeping gesture away from the lips to the listeners, opening your fingers and mouth as you do so.
- ✪ For the confession, explain that pieces of paper will be distributed so that everyone can 'write' their silent confession using their finger as a 'pen'.
- ✪ For intercessory prayer, children will be invited to pray for the Church (picture), for the world (point to place on globe), and for people (in the mind's eye put a person's image in the blank photo frame). Place a pebble at the foot of each item as a symbol of prayer.
- ✪ During the singing of the Gloria, bubbles will be blown, bells will be rung and everyone else can raise their arms in the air as a gesture of praise.
- ✪ At the distribution, bread will be broken and baskets will be passed around. The children are to take a piece of bread and hold it until everyone can eat together.
- ✪ 'Wine' will be passed in a goblet with a serviette. The children are to take a sip, wipe the goblet clean and then pass it to the next person.
- ✪ At the end, everyone will link in a line by putting one hand on the shoulder of the person in front, and then leave the room.

Application

Arrange the children on chairs in a horseshoe shape, with the altar at the open end. The leader sits at the apex of the horseshoe. Ask two children to carry the box with the symbols to the altar. Lay the tablecloth and unpack all the items on to the altar. Light the candles. The other box with the props goes to the leader. After a few moments' silence, go through the eucharistic service in the sequence below.

1. **Greeting**: Gesture to everyone to stand. Greet by bowing (Chinese style). Go among the children, using the Holy Spirit symbol to signify 'His spirit is with us'.

2. **Confession**: Gesture to sit. Hand out pieces of paper. Silently invite everyone to use his or her fingers to 'write' a confession. Use the basket to gather up the paper. Offer the basket of 'confessions' at the altar. Then take the bundle of paper and tear it up. Throw the paper away to the other side of the altar.

3. **Gloria**: Everyone stands with arms in the air. Ask some children to ring bells and blow bubbles.

4. **Ministry of the word**: Take the Bible from the altar. Open it as if to read. Using the suggested gestures, signify 'God speaks to us' and 'We listen to God'. Give the Bible to a child to place back on the altar.

5. **Creed**: For 'I believe in God the Father who made the world', use the suggested gestures by pointing to yourself, your head and your heart, and then to God. Next, fully inflate the globe of the world.

For 'I believe in Jesus who saved the world', use the suggested gestures by pointing to yourself, your head and your heart, and then to Jesus. Then ask a child to throw the globe, aiming past you. Save the shot in the same way that a goalkeeper would save a goal. Put the globe on the altar.

For 'I believe in the Holy Spirit who gives power to the people of God', use the suggested gestures for self, head, heart and Holy Spirit, then flex bicep muscles and gesture to everyone.

6. **Intercessions**: Invite everyone to take a pebble and then pray for the church, the world and each other as in the Introduction above.

7. **The Peace**: Put a peace garland over the head of the person on either side of you. They then pass the garland from one person to another. When everyone has received and passed the garlands, put them on the altar.

8. **'Consecration' of bread and wine**: First of all, take the bread. Wrap the loaf symbolically with a white cloth (like swaddling bands). Hold it like a baby in your arms. Put the crown of thorns on the head of the 'baby'. Hold the 'baby' high in the air in front of the altar. Take off the crown and place it on the altar. Unwrap the bread and raise it high in the air in front of the altar, place it on altar and then use the Holy Spirit gesture over it.

Next, take the bottle of 'wine' and insert the corkscrew into the bottle. Gently screw it in. As the arms of the corkscrew come up, show the children what is happening. Stop when the arms reach a horizontal position. Show the bottle again and then raise it up high in front of the altar. (The corkscrew is a reminder of Jesus on the cross.) Put the bottle on the altar and loop the crown of thorns over the raised corkscrew. Then use the Holy Spirit gesture over it. Finally, open the bottle and pour some 'wine' into each of the two goblets.

Take the bread and dramatically break it. Divide it into the two baskets and pass the baskets to either side of the horseshoe. Wait until everyone has taken a piece of bread before eating the bread together. Then pass one of the goblets to the person on your left and one to the person on your right. Let the children each take a sip, refilling the goblet as required, and wiping the lip of the goblet after each child has drunk.

9. **After Communion**: Inflate the balloon and draw a red heart on it. Signify 'God loves us' by pointing to God, to the red heart, and then to everyone.

10. **Blessing**: Use a traditional gesture of blessing by signing the cross to everyone.

11. **Dismissal**: Put one of the peace garlands on the nearest person. Gesture to them to leave the room, by pointing to the door. Everyone links arms and slowly processes out in sequence to signify going out into the world. Exit in silence.

Optional extras

1 A windmill can be blown as an alternative symbol for the Holy Spirit.
2 A ceramic dove of peace (or equivalent) can be used instead of a garland to signify the peace.
3 If available, a manger, placed in front of the altar, can be used to emphasize that the wrapped bread represents the baby Jesus.

Assembly Two: Teamwork, harvest-tide and combine harvesters

This worship is action-based and involves all the children. A combine harvester is constructed out of human bodies and put to work. Other participants in the act of worship make the noises of the machine parts. The aim is to get the children to think about the need for us all to work together as a team: successful harvests demand teamwork. It is particularly appropriate for worship during harvest-time.

You will need:
✤ A table, a tablecloth and a candle.
✤ An image of a combine harvester to project.

Suggested opening music and entrance

✪ Any harvest-time music or a recording of a machine noise

Christian greeting

Leader: God is building a people of power.
Response: And making a people of praise.

Introduction

Explain how farmers use combine harvesters to gather in their ripe corn. Refer to the image. Then explain the following facts.

- The 'chines' at the front of the machine grab the corn stalks and draw them into the machine.
- The corn seeds are shaken off and blown out through a spout into a trailer running alongside.
- The stalks of straw are then pumped out of the back of the machine on to the ground.
- Controlling all this, of course, is the driver.

Construct a human combine harvester involving ten children.

You will need:
- Either a tall child or one of the adults to be the driver. This person stands upright, facing forwards, holding an imaginary steering wheel.
- A tall child to be the corn spout. This person stands behind the steering wheel, facing sideways and 'vibrating' with his or her arms outstretched together horizontally to form the corn spout.
- Two children to be the chines. These two people kneel in front of the steering wheel, facing forwards. Their hands and forearms need to make a rolling, tumbling action, grabbing the corn stalks and pulling them into the machine.

❖ Two children to be the straw dispensers. These two people kneel behind the corn spout, facing backwards. Their hands and forearms need to make a rhythmical pushing action as if forcing the straw out of the machine.

❖ Four children to be the wheels. These people kneel, two on each side, facing outwards. Each child then joins his or her hands together and rotates their arms in a circular motion to simulate a turning wheel. (Make sure the 'wheel' turns in the right direction!)

All ten participants need to be clustered reasonably closely together so that they can be perceived as a single unit. Ask them all to practise their arm movements for just a few seconds and then to be still.

Divide everyone else, both adults and children, into four groups. Each group needs to make one of the following sound effects for the machine. When everyone has practised their sound effect, ask them to be quiet.

1 The engine noise (use your imagination!)
2 The rotating chines (chunk, chunk)
3 The corn spout (hiss, hiss)
4 The straw dispensers (shush, shush)

Start up the combine harvester. Ask the driver to press an imaginary button to start the engine. Commence the engine noise (group 1). Ask the two 'chines' to begin their arm movements. Commence the rotating chine noise (group 2). Start the corn spout noise (group 3). The 'corn spout' child can now begin to vibrate. Ask the two 'straw dispenser' children to start their arm movements. Commence the straw dispensing noise (group 4).

Get the combine harvester moving. The driver needs to say 'move' as an imaginary lever is pulled. All the component children forming the combine harvester move in the forward direction of the machine. This, of course, will include the four 'wheel' children shuffling sideways on their feet, and the two 'straw dispenser' children shuffling backwards on their knees (since they are all facing in different directions). All the sound effects and the arm actions must continue as the human machine moves forward.

When the machine reaches the edge of the working space, ask the driver to turn the whole machine around and work back in the opposite direction. Keep the arm actions and sound effects going.

Stop the machine and systematically turn off the component parts. Pause for a time of reflection. Then question the children about how it felt to be part of the machine. Tease out the fact that sometimes it is quite difficult to work together. Often, we are pulled apart. Talk about how a successful harvest is dependent upon members of the community working together: seed producers, fertiliser companies, transport and fuel industries, financial institutions, machine manufacturers, farm labourers, flour mills, bakeries and so on. Stress the fact that if one component fails, every component suffers.

Prayer

Light the candle before praying the following prayer.

Dear God, we thank you for the harvest and for all the food we eat. We thank you, too, for all the people in various industries who have worked together to make the harvest possible. We ask now that you will help us to work together more effectively as a team and that you will bless all those agencies working together to bring relief to people who are starving and in need of help. Amen

Suggested closing song

For I'm building a people of power (HON 135)

Dismissal

Leader: We are the body of Christ.
Response: Let us work together to do his will.

Suggested music to exit

Exit to any harvest-time music or a recording of a machine noise.

Optional extras

1 Reflect on the combine harvester as a manufactured machine. It is made using various components from different industries, such as steel, glass, plastic, rubber, paint, fuel and so on. All these component parts are brought together into the one machine; if one part fails, the whole machine fails.
2 Ask a local farmer to talk about the teamwork needed to bring in the harvest.

The journey of life: patterns for living

Key focus: Living life as a disciple of Jesus today

Background information for the teacher

Christians, whatever their denomination, believe that they are part of God's family. They realize that they need to work together for God and to show their love for all God's creation. Jesus showed his love for God and his love for God's people in practical ways, such as teaching, healing, helping and welcoming. Christians today try to do the same.

There are many examples of Christians putting their love into action. It might be babysitting for someone, or it might involve organizing a huge charity event for overseas aid. The Christian faith is best expressed in action, and there are many people willing to talk about their commitment, belief and lifestyle as members of the Christian Church. One way is to help the many charitable organizations, either by donation or by actively working for them— for example, collecting money or goods, or working on projects such as soup kitchens for the homeless or digging irrigation systems overseas. There are a number of charities that carry out such work and they usually have local educational contacts willing to come into school to talk to pupils.

Belief in Jesus, and belonging to the Church, therefore carry a firm commitment to live according to fundamental Christian values, such as forgiveness, stewardship and compassion. These Christian values are gospel values extolled in the teachings of Jesus himself.

The Lord's Prayer is a prayer that helps Christians to focus on their past behaviour ('Forgive us our sins as we forgive those who have sinned against us'), on their present needs ('Give us today our daily bread') and their hopes for the future ('Lead us not into temptation'). Behind it all, of course, is the fundamental desire expressed by the words 'Your kingdom come, your will be done on earth as it is in heaven'. It is by living out Christian values that Christians play their part in bringing into being the kingdom of God here on earth, today.

These Christian values are also expressed in Jesus' summary of the law. When a Pharisee asked Jesus what was the most important commandment in the law, he answered, '"Love the Lord your God with all your heart, soul, and mind." This is the first and most important commandment. The second most important commandment is like this one. And it is, "Love others as much as you love yourself"' (Matthew 22:37–39).

Therefore, at the heart of Christian discipleship is the command to love others as much as we love ourselves. This love must be expressed in actions as well as with words. Jesus made this quite clear in his teaching in Matthew 5:1–12. The passage has become known as the Beatitudes (blessings), and in it are included declarations such as 'God blesses those people who are merciful. They will be treated with mercy!' (v. 7) and 'God blesses those people who make peace. They will be called his children!' (v. 9).

Such commands and declarations by Jesus on how Christians should live inform the behaviour of the Church as a whole and of Christians as individuals.

Exploring the story

Read Luke 10:25–37. Jesus was once asked 'Who are my neighbours?' by a teacher of the Jewish law. He answered the question with a story about a man who was travelling from Jerusalem to Jericho. On the way, the man was attacked by robbers, who beat him and left him to die. Jesus explained that, when they saw the man lying in the road, both a priest and a temple helper (known as a Levite) walked past and left him. It was a foreigner from Samaria—someone who would have been despised by the Jewish people at the time—who cared for the man by tending to his wounds and taking him to an inn to receive help. Jesus then asked the teacher of the Jewish law which of these three people was a real neighbour to the man. When the teacher answered, 'The one who showed pity', Jesus told him to go and do the same. This story is known as the story of the good Samaritan.

Introductory questions about the story

❂ What was Jesus trying to explain to the teacher of Jewish law in this story?

Introductory tasks

❂ Find out what the road from Jerusalem to Jericho might have looked like. Imagine the scene. Then find out about priests and Levites at the time and their temple duties. Write a modern-day story or play based on the story of the good Samaritan to help explain Jesus' teaching. Think about the setting and the characters you might include.

- Read Matthew 5:1–11 and 43–48. This passage is part of the Sermon on the Mount, in which Jesus taught his followers how God wants people to behave. Read each of the verses carefully. You might also look at various translations in different Bibles and then try to make a PowerPoint presentation to reflect the sentiments contained in this important teaching for Christians today. Your PowerPoint presentation could be used in collective worship.
- Explore a selection of Christian hymns. Find out which ones teach Christians how to behave—for example, 'When I needed a neighbour' by Sydney Carter (HON 548).
- Find out about Christian charitable organizations around the world and the work that they do to follow the teachings of Jesus.

Key symbols in the story

Oil and wine

Oil and wine were used as antiseptic for treating wounds.

Priest and Levite

These symbols represented the established religion and practice of the time. The temple hierarchy was very complex, but both the priest and the Levite administered God's law and were symbols of authority.

Samaritan

A race discriminated against and hated by the Jewish people.

Inn

A symbol of hospitality, safety and nourishment.

Coins

A sign of compassion and generosity.

Road

The journey on the road from Jerusalem to Jericho was often hard and the environment hostile, which made travelling difficult. The road therefore symbolizes following in the footsteps of Jesus and the journey as a Christian.

Understanding the story through the senses

Sight

Many artists have tried to capture the story of the Good Samaritan. Find an image of Vincent Van Gogh's painting of *The Good Samaritan*. If you look closely at the picture you will see both the priest and the temple helper (Levite) walking away from the scene. One appears to be reading a book, possibly a religious text. Meanwhile, the Samaritan is struggling to help the injured man on to the horse. Explore other artworks depicting this story. Which one do you think conveys the message that Jesus was trying to put across? Reflect on other images to show Christians putting the teachings of Jesus into action.

Sound

Imagine that this story had been made into a short film. Consider the sound effects that you would have added to the script. Would it have been silent? Would the injured man have been crying in pain? The road from Jerusalem to Jericho is very rocky. How might it have sounded as the robbers approached? What about the sounds of the horses' hooves as the Samaritan stopped to help? What would have been the conversation that took place between the injured man and the Samaritan, and the Samaritan and the innkeeper or other characters in the story?

Smell

The story tells how the Samaritan treated the man's wounds with oil and wine. These substances would have been used as antiseptic at that time. Find a bottle of pure olive oil. Does it smell? Wine also has its own distinctive smell. Can you think of any other smells that might have been present? Not all of them would have been very pleasant. Christians today often go into very unpleasant places to follow Jesus' teachings. Can you think what or where some of these might be?

Touch

This story talks a lot about the sense of touch: from the bandits who physically beat up and robbed the man, to the Samaritan who must have gently bound up the injured man as he lay bleeding and dying. Touch can be used both to hurt and to reassure and heal. Think about the different ways in which we use our hands to touch. Are they used for good or evil? Think about the different ways in which Christians throughout the world use their hands in a good and positive way.

Taste

Many images of the story of the good Samaritan show the Samaritan giving the injured man something to drink. The road is a long, dusty one, close to the desert. It would have been hot and sandy. Lying injured, the man must have been very thirsty. The Samaritan took the man to an inn and paid the innkeeper to take care of him. This would have involved food and drink. Basic food, such as bread, and water are so important to sustain life. Think about how Christians help in times of drought and famine across the world.

A focus table of reflection for the classroom

Ask the children to research some Christian charitable organizations and the work that they do, such as Christian Aid, Tear Fund, Barnardo's, Oxfam, USPG, CAFOD, CMS, The Children's Society and The Salvation Army. Decide upon a charity that they wish to support (perhaps one that the school already supports). Ask the children to think of exciting fund-raising activities to support the charity of their choice.

Make a classroom display of the work that the charity carries out, both in the United Kingdom and across the world. On a table, have some grains of rice and some dry earth as a reminder of how fortunate many of us are in the Western world. Ask the children to write some prayers for those in need. Each day, light a candle and ask the children to read their prayers. If the children raise some money, you might invite someone from the charity to talk about their work and receive the donation.

Reflecting on the story

Assembly One: Sharing in a caring community

The following outline will enable pupils to appreciate how well off we are in relation to communities where there is famine and drought. It will also challenge them about whether they could do more in charitable support of others.

You will need:
- A large table with a cloth and a candle.
- A tray.
- A bag of uncooked rice.
- A few handfuls of dry soil.
- A stopwatch.
- An image showing famine relief.
- A box full of preserved food items.

Suggested opening music and entrance

○ 'Do they know it's Christmas?' by Band Aid

Project the image on to a screen.

Christian greeting

Leader: Let us come before God with thanksgiving in our hearts.
Response: As we remember all those who are hungry this day.

Introduction

Unpack the box of food items to remind the children of the immense variety of goods that we have available on our shelves today. Place items on the table. Contrast that sight with the image on the screen illustrating famine relief. Explain that many communities in famine-stricken countries rely on relief aid provided by charitable agencies, but that relief aid is rarely adequate. Individuals have to compete for food and it is a fight for survival. To illustrate this, explain that you want the children to imagine they are in a village overseas, experiencing severe famine.

Application

Choose two children to play the part of starving villagers. Explain that when lorries of relief aid arrive in a village, everyone clamours to get at the sacks of rice. Often, rice spills on the ground and individuals grovel in the dust to scoop up what they can. Now act this out in the form of a competition between the two chosen children.

Put two handfuls of dry soil on a tray and add a handful of dried rice. Mix the soil and rice together. Place the tray on the ground. Now tell the two children that they have one minute to pick out as many rice grains as they can from the soil. Time them. Then count the number of grains that each child has collected and declare the winner. Explain the stark reality that in a real-life situation the child who collected most rice is the one most likely to survive the famine. The one with the least will be the one most likely to die.

Discuss with the children their reactions to what they have seen, as well as any ideas they might have to overcome the problems of famine and unequal wealth in our world.

Prayer

As you put the tray of earth and rice on the table, light the candle and pray the following prayer.

Dear God, we pray for all those who are hungry today and for all those in relief agencies who work so hard to get food to them. Please show us what we can do to give support. Help us never to take our own meals for granted. Amen

Suggested closing song

When I needed a neighbour (HON 548)

Dismissal

Leader: Let us go to the world.
Response: And care for those in need.

Suggested music to exit

☉ 'Feed the world'

Optional extras

1 Hold this worship during Christian Aid Week and invite someone to talk about the work of Christian Aid.
2 Identify the places of origin of the food items and locate them on a map of the world. Thank God for the variety of food we enjoy.

Assembly Two: Discarding rubbish and recycling what is good

This act of worship is designed to encourage children to reflect upon the rotten things of life that they would like to leave behind for a fresh start. In contrast, they will be encouraged to reflect upon the times they have followed Christian ideals and upheld Christian values. These are the things that they are encouraged to recycle as they journey onwards into the future. This is an excellent basis for an end-of-year leavers' service.

You will need:
✤ Two clean wheelie bins, one marked 'rubbish' and the other 'recyclable'. Each bin should be lined with a clean plastic bag to keep everything hygienic.
✤ A bag of 'clean' rubbish, such as paper, cardboard, plastic wrappings, washed aluminium cans and so on.

✤ A flipchart with two sheets, the top sheet labelled 'rubbish' and the second sheet labelled 'recyclable'.
✤ Party poppers or, better still, a giant popper such as one might use at a wedding.
✤ A table with a tablecloth and a candle.

Suggested opening music and entrance

◉ 'Earth song' by Michael Jackson

Christian greeting

Leader: Come, let us give thanks to God for the past.
Response: And offer him our hopes for the future.

Introduction

Explain to the children that they are going to reflect upon all their good experiences to date and then contrast them with past mistakes. Then explain that they are going to look forward to the future, thinking about Christian values that they have found helpful and would like to carry forward.

Application

Bring out the two wheelie bins. Empty the sack of 'rubbish' on the floor. Invite children to place the rubbish items into either the rubbish bin or the recyclable bin. Emphasize that there are some bits from the past that we want to dispose of and some things that are worth recycling.

Encourage the children to think about their past. Invite them to think about the rotten bits, such as bullying, lying, jealousy, greed, hatred, anger or laziness. Next, ask them to name these negative things, emphasizing that their suggestions can be general rather than personal. Write the suggestions up on the flipchart sheet labelled 'rubbish'. Tear off the sheet and cast it into the rubbish bin.

Now encourage the children to think about good things from the past that they value, such as honesty, caring, friendship, hope, understanding of God, commitment, forgiveness, love of learning, peace and trust. Tear this list off, carefully fold it up and place it into the 'recyclable' bin. Emphasize that these are all things that we cherish and would like to hang on to. Put the two wheelie bins by the table and light the candle.

Prayer

Explain that you will be using a party popper as a prayer tool. Ask each child to think of one particular item from the recycling list that they would like to offer to God in prayer. Ask them to 'place' that request into a streamer emerging from the popper as a prayer to God. Pause. Release the popper. Repeat with each child, as desired. If you are using one large party popper, release the popper after all the children have contributed their prayer items.

Suggested closing song

One more step along the world I go (HON 405)
A new commandment I give unto you (MP 1)

Dismissal

Leader: Let us go in peace to love and serve the Lord.
Response: As we follow in his footsteps and follow in his ways.

Suggested music to exit

❂ 'Earth song' by Michael Jackson

✣

Resources

Music CDs

Most of the recorded music recommended in this book can be readily found on CD. Suggested sources are given below, chapter by chapter.

The story of creation

R. Strauss, *Also Sprach Zarathustra*, Berlin Philharmonic Orchestra, cond. Herbert von Karajan, (Universal Classics, 1995), ASIN B000001GQT.

E. Grieg, 'Morning mood' from *Peer Gynt Suite No 1*, on *Grieg Piano Music Vol. 4* (Naxos, 1995), ASIN B000001401.

F.J. Haydn, *The Creation* (Classics for Pleasure, 2006), ASIN B000JJ4G5M.

J. Rutter, 'All things bright and beautiful', on *The John Rutter Collection*, Cambridge Singers (Universal Classics, 2002), ASIN B00006LIEZ.

The story of re-creation

'Nunc Dimittis', on *Light of the World*, The Abbey School Choir, Tewkesbury: visit www.signumrecords.com

'Abba, Father', on CD2, *More Best Worship Songs Ever* (Kingsway, 2005).

'Dear Lord and Father of mankind', on *Hymns and Psalms from Winchester*, Winchester Cathedral Choir: visit www.heraldav.co.uk.

Laurie London, *He's Got the Whole World in His Hands* (Bearf, 2003), ASIN B00005BGYA.

Louis Armstrong, *What a Wonderful World* (Universal/Island, 1999), ASIN B000026E1N.

The story of baptism

'Holy, holy, holy', on *23 Favourite Hymns*, Norwich Cathedral Choir: visit www.cathedral.org.uk.

The story of incarnation

Slade, 'Merry Christmas everybody', *Wall of Hits* (Polydor, 1991), ASIN B000007UFW.

'Hark! the herald-angels sing' and 'The first Nowell', on *Essential Carols*, King's College Choir, Cambridge (Universal Classics, 2005), ASIN B000AAFH5I.

'We three kings of Orient are', on *Songs of Angels—Christmas Hymns and Carols*, Robert Shaw Chamber Singers (Telarc, 2001), ASIN B000003D0G.

The story of Lent

'As pants the hart for cooling streams', on *Hymns of Love, Hope and Joy*: visit www.thepriorysingersbelfast.com.

Saint-Saens, The *Carnival of the Animals*, City of Birmingham Symphony Orchestra (Classics for Pleasure, 2007), ASIN B000MCIB5W.

'Forty days and forty nights', on *Hills of the North, Rejoice* (The English Hymn 3), Wells Cathedral Choir (Hyperion, 2002), ASIN B00006GO6I.

'Father, hear the prayer we offer', on *Christ Triumphant* (The English Hymn 1), Wells Cathedral Choir (Hyperion, 1999), ASIN B000038I68

The story of Holy Week

A. Lloyd Webber, 'Pie Jesu', on *The Andrew Lloyd Webber Collection* (Xtra, 2005), ASIN B0007D55G4.

G. Allegri, 'Miserere mei', on *Allegri Miserere*, The Tallis Scholars, cond. Peter Phillips (Gimell, 2007), ASIN B000LXHFWC.

C. Franck, 'Panis angelicus', on *Best-Loved Wedding Music*, (Seraphim, 2000), ASIM B000000UXE.

J.S. Bach, *St Matthew Passion*, The Bach Choir (Universal Classics, 2006), ASIN B000J233L2.

The story of Easter

'Thine be the glory', on *Lead Kindly Light* (The English Hymn 5), Wells Cathedral Choir (Hyperion, 2004), ASIN B0002JEK7S.

J. Rutter, 'The Lord bless you and keep you', on Bryn Terfel, *A Song in My Heart* (UCJ, 2007), ASIN B000QFAH9S.

'This joyful Eastertide', on *Music for Holy Week*, King's College Choir, Cambridge (EMI, 1994), ASIN B000002S5K.

The story of Pentecost

J. Sibelius, *Finlandia*, Iceland Symphony Orchestra, cond. Petri Sakari (Naxos, 1999), ASIN B00001NTM2.

R. Vaughan Williams, 'The lark ascending', on *Symphony No. 2 'London' and The Lark Ascending*, Royal Philharmonic Orchestra, cond. Andre Previn (Telarc, 2002), ASIN B000003CU5.

The journey of life: belonging and believing

'Dem bones, dem bones, dem dry bones', on *Dem Bones*, Carla Cook (Maxjazz, 2002), ASIN B0000589E1.

'Rhythm of life', on *Sweet Charity* (Columbia Broadway Masterworks, 1999), ASIN B000026C2A.

'Sunrise sunset', on *Fiddler on the Roof 30th Anniversary Edition* (EMI, 2001), ASIN B00005OB07.

The journey of life: patterns for living

Band Aid 20, 'Do they know it's Christmas?' (single) (Mercury, 2004), ASIN B0006I0S6C.

M. Jackson, 'Earth song' (single) (Epic, 2006), ASIN B000CNET98.

Song books

Church Family Worship, Hodder and Stoughton (ISBN 978-0340393956).

Hymns Old and New (New Anglican Edition), Kevin Mayhew (ISBN 978-862098063).

Mission Praise, Collins (ISBN 978-0007193448).

Wild Goose Songs Volume 3, Wild Goose Publications (ISBN 978-0947988340).

Teaching resources

The Salisbury diocesan website www.saled.org provides additional images that may be used to inspire both teachers and pupils.

Stefano Zuffi, *Gospel Figures in Art* (translated by Thomas Hartmann), Getty Trust, 2002.

John Bowker, *The Complete Bible Handbook*, Dorling Kindersley, 1998.

Susan Wright, *The Bible in Art*, New Line Books, 1998.

Margaret Cooling, *Jesus through Art*, RMEP in association with National Gallery Publications Ltd, 1998.

Lilian Weatherley and Trevor Reader, *Teaching Christianity at Key Stage 2*, The National Society/Church House Publishing, 2001.

Paul Forsey, *The Life of Jesus: Through the eyes of an artist*, Barnabas, 2004.

David Barton with Jo Fageant, *The Life of Jesus: Through the eyes of an artist* Teacher's Guide, Barnabas, 2004.

Rhona Davies, *The Barnabas Schools' Bible*, Barnabas, 2007.

The Life of Jesus
Through the eyes of an artist

Based on original paintings by Paul Forsey

This distinctive book provides a unique opportunity to discover the story of Jesus' life through the evocative contemporary work of a single artist. Within its pages, 22 key events in the life of Jesus have been interpreted through the artist's vibrant artwork, accompanied by the related Bible texts in a modern translation.

ISBN 978 1 84101 330 5   £12.99

The Life of Jesus
Teacher's Guide

David Barton with Jo Fageant

This teaching resource is designed to accompany the illustrated book. The material is organized in three sections: complementary narratives, accompanying notes and lesson planning guides. Assessment questions drawn from the QCA Level Descriptions for RE, are provided at the end of each unit to enable teachers to make assessments of pupils' learning.

ISBN 978 1 84101 331 2   £11.99

The Barnabas Schools' Bible

Rhona Davies

Illustrated by Marcin Piwowarski

This new Children's Bible includes stories chosen to cover all the main events, retold with a continuous thread.

There are 365 stories, one for every day of the year, each accompanied by Bible quotations from a real Bible translation, giving readers a taste of the language and style of the original texts.

The stylish illustrations illuminate and inform, while the easily accessible encyclopedia at the end of the book helps to explain the context and background of the stories. All combine to make this a useful and readable Bible for KS2 children.

ISBN 978 1 84101 564 4   £12.99

ORDER FORM

REF	TITLE	PRICE	QTY	TOTAL
330 5	The Life of Jesus	£12.99		
331 2	The Life of Jesus Teacher's Guide	£11.99		
564 4	The Barnabas Schools' Bible	£12.99		

POSTAGE AND PACKING CHARGES					Postage and packing:	
Order value	UK	Europe	Surface	Air Mail	Donation:	
£7.00 & under	£1.25	£3.00	£3.50	£5.50	**Total enclosed:**	
£7.01–£30.00	£2.25	£5.50	£6.50	£10.00		
Over £30.00	free	prices on request				

Name _____ Account Number _____

Address _____

_____ Postcode _____

Telephone Number _____ Email _____

Payment by: ❏ Cheque ❏ Mastercard ❏ Visa ❏ Postal Order ❏ Maestro

Card no. ☐☐☐☐ ☐☐☐☐ ☐☐☐☐ ☐☐☐☐

Expires ☐☐ ☐☐   Security code ☐☐☐   Issue no. ☐☐☐

Signature _____ Date _____

All orders must be accompanied by the appropriate payment.

Please send your completed order form to:
BRF, 15 The Chambers, Vineyard, Abingdon OX14 3FE
Tel. 01865 319700 / Fax. 01865 319701 Email: enquiries@brf.org.uk

❏ Please send me further information about BRF publications.

Available from your local Christian bookshop.   BRF is a Registered Charity

Resourcing **Collective Worship and Assemblies, RE, Festivals, Drama** and **Art** in primary schools

- Barnabas RE Days—exploring Christianity creatively
- INSET
- Books and resources
- www.barnabasinschools.org.uk

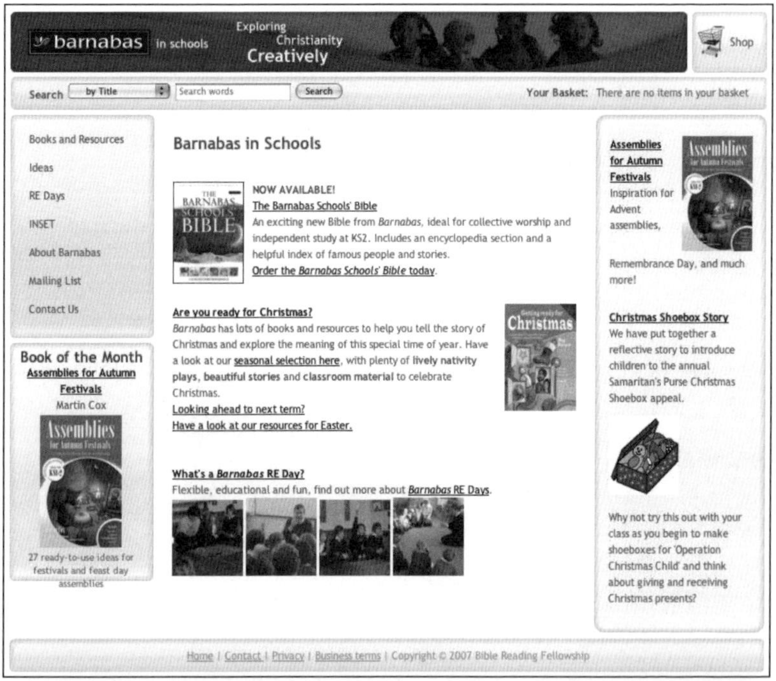

visit barnabas at www.barnabasinschools.org.uk

Barnabas is an imprint of brf

BRF is a Registered Charity